Growing Potatoes

*How to Grow Potatoes in Containers,
Raised Beds, Bags, the Ground and
More Along with Tips for Harvesting
and Storing*

Contents

Introduction

How often have you dragged home a sack of spuds from the grocery store and wished you had the room and the know-how to grow your own? Well, I'm here to tell you you can, and you don't need acres of land to do it, either.

Some people think that growing potatoes is no more difficult than just shoving a spud in the ground and watering it. Well, sure, you can do it that way, but don't expect to get a great crop out of it. Potato growing requires a little more involvement than that, and how you do it depends on where or what you are growing them in.

This book will walk you through everything you need to know about growing your own potatoes. It's the perfect guide for complete beginners, as it takes you through everything, one step at a time, and it's also ideal for those with a little more experience who want to make the most out of their space and learn a few more techniques to help them improve.

This book is written in simple language, with step-by-step instructions, and is very easy to understand. Each chapter is a guide on its own, so if you already have some experience, you can simply pick the chapter with the information you want without worrying about missing any vital information.

If you're ready to learn how to grow potatoes in your backyard or even on your balcony, let's dive in and see how it's done.

Chapter 1: An Introduction to Growing Potatoes

The potato - one of the humblest yet most diverse vegetables - can be traced back as far as 500 BC, with potato remains found in Ancient Chilean and Peruvian ruins. The Incas not only grew potatoes as a staple food, but they also worshipped them, even burying them with their dead. They filled bins with potatoes and concealed them, hidden away for times of famine or war. They dried potatoes to preserve them and carried them when they embarked on long journeys, eating them dry or soaking them in a stew. As they still do today, the Incas called their potatoes "papas," and, in ancient times, they had dark purple skins with yellow flesh.

Historians say that the Incans used to say the following prayer to worship potatoes:

"O, Creator! Thou who givest life to all things and hast made men that they may live and multiply. Multiply also the fruits of the earth, the potatoes and other food that thou hast made, that men may not suffer from hunger and misery."

In 1532, the Spanish Conquistadors saw their first potato when they landed in Peru in search of Gold. In 1540, a Spanish Conquistador and historian, Pedro de Cieza, wrote the following about the potato in his Chronicles of Peru:

"In the vicinities of Quito, the inhabitants have with to the maize another plant that serves to support in great part their existence: the potatoes, that they are of the roots similar to the tubercoli, supplies of one rind more or little hard; when they come bubbled they become to hold like the cooked chestnuts; seccate to the sun call to them chuno and they are conserved for the use."

In 1565, Gonzalo Jiminez de Quesada, a Spanish conqueror, and explorer decided that he would take potatoes to Spain as he couldn't find any gold. Thinking they were a truffle, the Spanish named them "tartuffo," and they soon became standard on Spanish ships, especially after it was noted that sailors didn't get scurvy when they dined on potatoes.

In 1597, John Gerard, a British author, rare plant collector, and avid gardener received some potato plant roots from Virginia and managed to grow them quite successfully in his garden. In his book, The Herball, he described the potato root as "thick, large and tuberosa" and of different shapes and sizes and named them "potatoes of Virginia." However, although this was the name used by early English botanists, the potatoes actually came from South America, not the US State of Virginia.

From there, the potato arrived in England and Italy in around 1585, in Germany and Belgium by 1587, in Austria in around 1588, and by 1600, they had arrived in France. Wherever it arrived, it was first seen as poisonous and strange, and some people even called it evil. In many countries, the potato was believed to be responsible for leprosy, syphilis, scrofula, narcosis, sterility, early death, and even rampant sexuality. Some people even claimed it destroyed the soil where it grew – and that is not so far from the truth, as you will discover later in the book. In fact, people were so opposed to the potato that, in Besancon, France, an edict was made stating that it was forbidden to cultivate it, and those caught doing so would face fines.

According to Irish legend, Spanish Armada ships carrying stores of potatoes wrecked off the coast in 1588, and some washed ashore. But it was in 1589 that the potato first arrived in Ireland, courtesy of British explorer and historian Sir Walter Raleigh. He planted the potatoes at Myrtle Grove, his Irish estate near Cork. Further legend says that he gifted Queen Elizabeth I with a potato plant, and the local gentry attended a royal banquet, where every course contained potato. However, the cooks had never seen potatoes before, much less learned how to cook them. Instead of preparing the potatoes, they threw them away and served boiled leaves and stems, which were highly poisonous. Everyone fell ill, and the potato was banned from the Royal Court.

The United States was introduced to the potato multiple times throughout the 1600s, but it wasn't until 1719 when Scotch-Irish immigrants began growing them in Londonderry, New Hampshire. From there, they spread across the entire country.

In 1771, a French military chemist and botanist, Antoine-Augustin Parmentier, participated in and won an Academy of Besancon-sponsored contest to find some form of food that could alleviate the trouble with famines, winning with a study on potatoes. A historical account claims he was a prisoner of the Prussians for no less than five times during the Seven Years War, and, each time, he had to survive on potatoes. Many dinners he was served were made up entirely of potato dishes, and many potato dishes in France are named in some way after him.

In 1785, Parmentier persuaded the then King of France, Louis XVI, to allow potatoes to be cultivated. The king granted him 100 acres of useless land outside of France, which Parmentier filled with potato plants. Troops were on hand to guard the field, raising curiosity among the people, who believed this must be a valuable crop to be so heavily guarded. Parmentier allowed the guards a night off, hoping that local farmers would enter the field to steal the potatoes. They did and consequently planted them on their own land, thus starting the habit of growing potatoes and eating them across France. Historians claim that the Queen of France, Marie Antoinette, would pin flowers from the potato plants in her hair, leading many other women of the same era to copy her.

Meanwhile, in Russia, the peasants would have nothing to do with the potato until the middle of the 1700s. They were sent free potatoes by Frederick the Great when the famine hit in 1774, but until soldiers arrived to persuade them, the peasants would still not touch them. Now, they are grown and eaten almost everywhere in Russia.

While potatoes grow everywhere in the USA, Idaho is the state most associated with them. In 1836, a Presbyterian missionary called Henry Harmon Spalding established a missionary in Lapwai to persuade the Nez Perce Indians to convert to Christianity. Wanting to show them how agriculture, rather than fishing or hunting, could help supply them with food, he planted potatoes, but his first crop failed. His second crop, the year after, was good but, because the Indians massacred all the people in another missionary group nearby, Spalding left, and potato growing ended for a while.

Between 1845 and 1849, the Irish suffered a great famine because many of their potato crops were ruined by disease. In around 1845, when the famine was at its height, more than a million people died of starvation. Many families were left with little choice but to continue struggling or emigrate. Many chose the latter, and towns were soon deserted, with shops closing everywhere after their owners emigrated. More than one and a half million Irish emigrated to Australia and North America, causing the population of Ireland to fall by over 50%.

In the 1800s, the potato was considered nothing more than animal feed by many Americans, and The Farmers Manual recommended it be grown for convenience near the hog's pens.

In 1862, Isabella Beeton wrote and published the Book of Household Management. In it, she wrote of the potato:

"It is generally supposed that the water in which potatoes are boiled is injurious; and as instances are recorded where cattle having drunk it were seriously affected, it may be well to err on the safe side and avoid its use for any alimentary purpose."

In 1872, Luther Burbank, an American horticulturist, developed the Russet Burbank potato, leading the potato industry in Idaho to soar. His development came about during his trials to improve the Irish potato, to ensure it was more resistant to the diseases that caused the famine, and the Burbank potato was introduced to Ireland. He sold the rights to the potato for $150 and used the money to travel to Santa Rosa in California. There he built his own nursery garden, including a large greenhouse and experimental farms that are now world-famous. By the time the 1900s rolled around, the Russet Burbank was becoming a popular choice in Idaho.

Today, we take the potato for granted. They grow everywhere, and there are literally hundreds of varieties. The potato is a common part of the Western diet, and it's easy to forget that it has really only been used in the Western world for a few hundred years.

Biological Classification and Structure

The potato, scientifically known as Solanum tuberosum, is an annual plant. That means it completes its entire growing and fruiting cycle within the year, dying off at the end, leaving you to start the following year again.

It is a part of the Nightshade family, the same one that contains tomatoes, eggplants, peppers, and so on. The potato is grown for its edible, starchy tubers and is now one of the main crops grown across the world, be it on farms or in people's backyards.

They are incredibly diverse in how they are prepared for eating – baked or boiled whole, mashed, chipped, etc. But they are also ground down into potato flour, used as sauce thickeners, and in baking. Additionally, the tubers are easy to digest and packed with protein, vitamin C, niacin, and thiamine.

The potato is from the genus Solanum which includes over 150 species that bear swollen tubers. The leaves are compound and arranged spirally, each one about 20-30 cm long and having one terminal leaflet and up to four pairs of leaflets.

POTATO PLANT

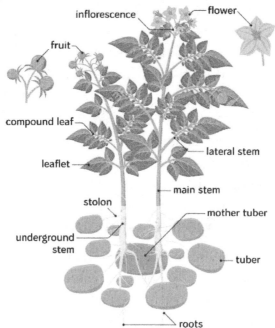

The flowers are yellow, white, or lavender/purple and have yellow stamens with fused flowers. Towards the end of their life, they will bloom, producing a small berry, which is poisonous, containing many seeds.

Under the ground, the stems extend into another structure called a stolon, the ends of which enlarge to form tubers. A single plant can have as many as 30 tubers of different shapes and sizes, ranging from 10 oz. all the way up to over 3 lbs. in weight. The skin on the tubers can be brown and white, through to yellow, to red or purple, depending on the variety grown, and flesh is typically white or yellow – some can be purple, but not many.

These tubers have buds on them, known as eyes, formed in the axils where leaf growth is aborted, leaving scars. The buds sprout clones of the main plant, which allows growers to propagate the characteristics they want in a potato. This is typically used in commercial settings, but this has resulted in a decrease in genetic diversity, leading to some of the more popular potato varieties being more susceptible to disease and pests.

8 Reasons Why You Should Grow Potatoes

If you were told you had to pick a single crop to help feed your family during hard times, you could do much worse than choosing the potato. Humble as they are, they are absolute superstars in the toughest of times.

These eight reasons tell you exactly why you should grow potatoes in your own backyard.

1. Potatoes are simple to grow, and you need no special machinery or equipment to process them. You can easily grow potatoes in your own garden with the smallest amount of labor and care. Unlike grain crops, you need not mill, combine, thresh, or process potatoes in any other way – simply dig them up, brush off the dirt and cook them.

2. They are one of the most nutritious vegetables. While potatoes have something of a rep, especially among the low-carb crowd, they are absolute powerhouses in terms of nutrients. One mid-sized potato can provide you with all the Vitamin B6 and Vitamin C you need in a day, plus nearly half of the daily recommended amount of potassium. They also contain folate, magnesium, thiamin, niacin, manganese, magnesium, and many more minerals and are a great source of fiber.

3. They are a healthy alternative to beans, grains, and pasta. Lots of pre-packaged foods are full of beans and grains, but not everyone can or wants to eat them. Potatoes are much easier to digest - they don't need soaking for long periods like beans and grains do -, especially for those who are intolerant or sensitive to gluten, so potatoes are the answer.

4. Say you find yourself in a TEOTWAWKI (the end of the world as we know it) situation. Or perhaps something not quite so desperate, but in a situation where you find yourself doing more manual work and having to grow your own food. Potatoes offer the best and easiest way of surviving as they require little effort and give you all the calories and nutrients you need.

5. You need little space. If you have a small backyard or even live in an apartment with a small balcony, you can still grow potatoes. You don't need a garden - they grow in bins, tubs, boxes, sacks, buckets, pretty much anything.

6. Provided they are stored properly, potatoes can be stored for months. We'll talk more about this later as there are some dos and don'ts, such as not storing potatoes near onions or garlic.

7. You can dehydrate potatoes. This is for those with limited storage space – simply scrub the potatoes clean, slice them, and pop them in a dehydrator or an oven. You can store them in airtight tubs for a long time – done properly – dehydrated potatoes can last for up to ten years!

8. Last, there are so many ways to prepare potatoes you simply cannot get bored with them. You can boil, mash, bake, fry, scallop them, and more. You can even make potato flour, potato dumplings, fries, potato pancakes, or even vodka for the more adventurous among you.

Whatever you choose to grow this year, make sure the potato is among your crops. It's the one food you can rely on!

Chapter 2: 40 Things to Know About Planting Potatoes

This chapter will go over some of the things you need to know about planting potatoes. Although some people will tell you you can just stick a spud in the ground, and it will grow, the process involves a little more than that if you want a successful crop. Let's dive in.

Growing Conditions

The weather plays a huge factor in the success of your crops, and the potato growing season must be cool and free of frost. In the hottest summers, you can grow potatoes and in spring, summer, and fall.

Your potatoes can be planted four to six weeks before the last frost in the spring and any time after the soil has reached 40°F or 4.4°C.

You can plant potatoes before the last frost because the actual seed won't be affected – unless your ground freezes to a foot or two below the surface (in which case, you won't be planting them anyway!). It is the green shoots that the frost can affect, and these can take a few weeks to show.

Depending on the variety you choose to grow, your plants will need between 75 and 135 frost-free days to reach optimum harvest levels.

Potatoes planted in the late winter or early spring should be harvested before temperatures reach 80°F or 27°C.

Potatoes do not like dry soil or extreme heat. They need plenty of water to form the tubers, and heat can discolor the flesh.

Where to Plant Your Spuds

Potatoes need full sun to grow and will not thrive in shaded areas.

They must be planted in well-drained and fertile soil, with lots of organic matter in it. A few inches of well-rotted manure or aged compost can be added to your growing area before you plant.

The soil should be loosened to around 18 inches or 45 cm deep if planting straight into the ground, or you can plant in containers, raised beds, or in mounds – all of these will be discussed later in the book.

Never plant potatoes where the soil is made of clay, heavily compacted, or is always soaking wet. Clay soil becomes rock-hard when it dries, stopping water from being absorbed and the tubers from growing.

Try not to plant in sandy soil as it drains water too quickly and, unless you water frequently, this results in drought stress.

Potatoes prefer soil with a pH of 5.0 to 5.5. While alkaline soil is great for a bigger crop, it does increase the risks of potato scab, a disease affecting the potato skin.

Improve the soil quality using aged compost – digging a couple of inches into the top 6-8 inches of topsoil can help with moisture retention, ensuring that enough moisture is maintained, but the excess can drain away. Plus, compost has certain nutrients that feed the potatoes, leading to a good, healthy harvest.

If your soil lacks nutrients, use a good quality fertilizer. Typically, a 10-10-5 or 5-10-5 blend works well and should be applied at 1.5 lbs. per 50 square feet. Potatoes require three primary nutrients - nitrogen, phosphorus, and potassium, otherwise known as NPK. The numbers relate to each nutrient's percentages, so 10-10-5 would be 10% each of nitrogen and phosphorus and 5% potassium. Once the potato plants have reached 4-6 inches in height, apply a second round of fertilizer at 1 lb. per 50 feet. This second application should be fed about 6 inches away from your plants and then immediately watered in.

Overly wet soil can cause your plants to rot, but potatoes need not be watered every day, contrary to popular belief. Deep watering once a week with about an inch of water is sufficient - this will penetrate the soil down to about 6 inches. You can also place a 2-4-inch layer of mulch or straw over the soil to help retain moisture and protect any potatoes that form close to the surface from being exposed to the sun - sun exposure turns the potatoes green, rendering them useless.

Planting Time

The right time to plant your potatoes will depend on the variety you choose, although many gardeners or farmers opt to plant a couple of different varieties. The potato varieties are classified by the time it takes to produce a harvest.

- **Early** - These varieties mature early, requiring between 5 and 90 days to come to harvest. These are a great choice for regions where the summers are very hot.

• **Midseason** – These need 90 to 135 days to come to harvest.

• **Lates** – Also known as long-season potatoes-need 135 to 160 days to harvest and are a great choice for regions that experience long, mild summers.

Here's when you need to plant them:

1. **Spring Planting** – These should be planted 3-4 weeks before the last frost. In Zone 7 or warmer, you can plant a second crop in the late summer, early fall. The spring planting should be timed so the last frosts cannot kill off the foliage. In regions where the summer is mild, you can plant earlies, mids, and lates in the spring, ensuring an extended harvest.

2. **Summer Planting** – These will be ready for harvesting in the fall, so plant no less than 12 weeks before the first frosts of fall are expected.

3. **Winter Planting** – In regions where the winters are mild and the summers are hotter, you can plant late-season spuds in the winter, and they will be ready for harvest in the spring before it gets too hot. Or you can plant earlies in the late summer and harvest them in the fall.

4. **Tropical/Sub-Tropical Planting** – You can grow potatoes all year round in these regions, although the best time is summer and fall, to ensure harvesting can be done before the rainy season hits.

Preparing Seed Potatoes

While some growers choose to grow potatoes from true seeds (more on that in a later chapter), most prefer to grow from seed potatoes.

Seed potatoes are small pieces of a potato or a whole potato.

The potato is not the root of the crop – it is a swollen stem.

Seed potatoes require at least one "eye" for successful sprouting – the eye is a small bud from which the sprouts grow, developing stems and leaves.

Always choose seed potatoes certified as disease-free. The ones you buy in the supermarket are typically treated with chemicals to stop them from sprouting. You can buy seed potatoes from garden centers or online.

Store your seed potatoes for up to 30 days in the refrigerator before you plant them.

If your seed potato has only one eye, plant it whole. If it has several, cut the potato into a few pieces, ensuring each piece has a couple of buds.

A couple of weeks before you plant your potatoes, set them somewhere warm and bright to encourage the sprouts – the temperature should be 65-70°F or 18-21°C.

If you cut your seed potatoes, do it two days before you plant them and use a sharp knife to do it.

Plant them in holes or trenches 34 inches or 7.5-10 cm deep. Cover the potatoes with 2 inches or 5 cm of soil.

Cut potatoes should be planted with the cut side facing downward.

If your soil is too heavy or wet to dig in, or if you prefer not to dig, place the potatoes on the surface and use a 4-6 inch or 10-15 cm deep layer of composted leaves or straw to cover them.

Planting and Spacing

- **Early varieties** – Sow these seed potatoes between 8 and 14 inches or 20 to 35 cm apart in a row. The rows should be spaced 12 to 18 inches or 30 to 45 cm apart.
- **Late varieties** – Sow these 13 to 14 inches or 30 to 35 cm apart, and the rows should be spaced 30 to 36 inches or 75 to 90 cm apart.
- When the potatoes begin sprouting, add another 2 inches of soil over the top.
- As the plants grow, add more soil, but always leave the top two leaf sets exposed.
- Never grow potatoes in the same place two years running and never place them where peppers and eggplants have been previously grown – these are all part of the same family and attract the same diseases and pests.

Growing Potatoes in Containers

- You can easily grow potatoes in containers, such as wooden boxes, sacks, half barrels, or even stacks of tires.
- The seed potatoes should be planted at the bottom of the container.
- As they grow, add more soil, leaving just the top couple of leaves exposed. Continue until the variety reaches its maturity or harvest day.

Companion Planting

Companion planting, as you will discover later, is important to all plants, not just potatoes. These are the general rules to follow to get the best out of your crop:

• Try to plant your potatoes near cabbage, corn, and beans, as these will encourage useful insects that help kill off the destructive ones.

• Don't plant them near squash, pumpkins, cucumber, tomatoes, sunflowers, or raspberries, as these plants attract the same pests that attack potatoes.

Follow these tips and all the other instructions in this book, and you should be able to successfully grow a great crop of spuds.

Chapter 3: Seed Potatoes – Varieties, Selection, and Preparation

Seed potatoes are potatoes specifically grown to be planted as a way of producing a crop of potatoes. I will be talking about actual seeds later on, but seed potatoes are the typical way that most growers and farmers plant their crops.

Potatoes are tubers, a type where the plant stores its energy so it can regrow the following year. If left in the ground, a potato will simply keep on sprouting but, for reasons we'll talk about later, this is not an ideal scenario.

Every potato will have numerous eyes, where new plants sprout from. The potatoes you purchase from the supermarket will sprout if you leave them long enough, but we don't recommend you plant those. There is every chance they have viral diseases or blight spores. Plus, many supermarket potatoes are treated with chemicals, and any resulting crop would be poor.

Purchasing proper seed potatoes is the way to go as they are certified as disease-free. Some places, such as Scotland in the UK, can supply these potatoes because their climate ensures virus and disease-spreading aphids cannot survive. Some varieties are produced as micro tubers or micro plants, produced in sterile lab conditions to ensure no diseases are present. However, this tends only to be done for the heirloom or heritage varieties, not the popular varieties that most people grow today.

You can also purchase dual plants, plants that produce potatoes and one other crop, such as the TomTater, but these plants require a good deal more care and feeding to produce good harvests of both vegetables.

When you shop for seed potatoes, it is much like shopping in the supermarket. The best candidates, in either case, are those that free of obvious blemishes, frostbite and are firm. You can purchase seed potatoes that have already begun sprouting but only buy those with short green stems. Those with long, spindly, white shoots should be avoided as the shoots are fragile and are unlikely to survive the planting process.

You can purchase seed potatoes from late winter through mid-spring, usually December/January through April. You can also order them online when you receive your new season seed catalogs.

The earlier you buy, the more choices you will have. While you may get a decent bargain, later on, you will be stuck with what is left.

Choosing Your Seed Potatoes

Which potato variety you choose will depend on numerous factors, not least where you live and the ideal varieties to grow in that region. Many regions have found that late blight disease affects many crops, sometimes reducing the yield and sometimes destroying the crop altogether. You need to consider blight-resistant varieties.

The main distinction between all varieties is the time taken to harvest – First Earlies, Second Earlies, Early Maincrop, and Late Maincrop. Salad potatoes tend to be earlies and are waxy potatoes.

- **First Earlies** – Plant from early through late spring. Early plantings need to have some protection from the frost, and they generally produce small potatoes known as new potatoes after about ten weeks.
- **Second Earlies** – Plant these a month later. They take around 13 weeks to produce, but the harvest is the same, small new potatoes.

The early and salad varieties are perfect for container growing.

Maincrops are better in the ground, and they produce a much larger harvest in about 20 weeks. These can be planted from March through late spring.

If you choose a second cropping variety, you can plant them in August, and they will be ready for harvest in the fall/winter, although they will need frost protection.

When you have decided on the type you want to buy, you need to decide on the variety and choose these based on what you want them for. Later, I will tell you about some of the more popular varieties but, generally, each variety has information on whether they are best for baking, frying, boiling, mashing, roasting, and so on.

You can also decide between heritage and modern varieties, those that produce different sizes, different skin or flesh colors, and so on. Most gardeners choose based on what grows in their region and which potatoes taste the best and store easily.

Choosing your seed potatoes is only the first step. The next step is to chit them (more on that later), which gives them a bit of a head start before you plant them and prevents the spindly, white, weak shoots that arise when stored in the dark.

Before You Start Growing

There are some things to consider when you decide which spuds to grow. First off, you need to consider what you want your potatoes for - fluffy mash, perfect chips, crispy roasties?

You might think that sounds daft, but not all potatoes are equal. Each variety has unique characteristics and traits, so some are better suited than others for certain things.

This all comes down to the amount of starch in each variety, not to mention sugar levels. The starch determines the fluffiness or flouriness of the potato and whether it breaks down when cooked or stays firm and waxy. The more starch, the more likely the potato will break down when cooked, making them perfect for baking, frying, and mashing.

Those with lower amounts of starch are waxier and tend to hold together when cooked, which makes them suitable for salads, stews, and soups.

One more difference between the varieties is the size of the potato - early potatoes tend to be smaller than the maincrops or lates, although the fingerling variety does come in both small and large varieties. The potatoes you buy as "new" are not a specific variety. They are just early potatoes harvested when they are small.

Top 11 Varieties to Grow at Home

Whether you want a thin-skinned red potato, a waxy, yellow one, or something in purple, these 11 varieties will cover your needs.

The Daisy Gold

The Daisy Gold variety is one of the best all-around potatoes, with moist and flaky flesh, perfect for baking, boiling, and mashing. It has a cheerful color, is highly vigorous, and is resistant to viruses. Most seed potatoes have up to five eyes and yield between 5 and 8 lbs. of potatoes each. It also has a high resistance to nematodes.

The tubers will mature to harvest about 80 days after they are planted and are ready mid-season.

The Kennebec

Another popular all-rounder, the Kennebec, has thin but smooth skin and a creamy texture. And, because it keeps its shape when you cook it, it is perfect for curries, salads, stews, and soups, while its starch level ensures great frying and mashing.

If you choose to grow these, you will get a great yield of potatoes. It is also good for storage, so you can continue to enjoy your harvest for many months.

It is an early maincrop and ready to harvest about 80 days after planting. The Kennebec is resistant to black leg, late blight, and the A and Y potato viruses.

The Red Gold

If you want something with a unique taste, the Red Gold is for you. It offers a nutty taste like nothing you will ever taste in a supermarket potato and has yellow flesh with eyes the color of raspberries.

e

It is a northern European variety, a mid-season potato great for frying, mashing, roasting, and baking. The crop is ready to harvest after 90 days, but they are best for the short-term only and not suited to long-term storage.

The Red Pontiac

Another good all-rounder, the Pontiac is an early-season variety with thin skin, making it perfect for new or maincrop potatoes. Its flesh has a waxy texture, great for mashing, boiling, baking, roasting, and in salads. However, they are not good for frying.

Ready for harvest after 80 days, they are relatively tolerant to drought.

The Rio Grande Russet

These are the healthiest potatoes of all. Provided you consume the skin too, it has plenty of antioxidants and is highly nutritious. Like most russets, it has tasty skin and a fluffy, floury texture.

It is also a high-yield potato and low in starch, which means it is best suited to chipping, slicing, and in salads.

Mature potatoes are between 4 and 5 inches in length, and the skin is a rusty-brown color with white flesh. It is ready to harvest within 59 to 65 days.

The Magic Molly

One of the more enchanting potatoes, it probably won't suit traditionalists. With deep purple skin and flesh, its taste is as exotic and rich as its color, and it doesn't lose color when it is boiled. It is the perfect potato for grilling as it perfectly complements woody, warm smoky accents.

However, they do take longer to reach maturity, between 95 and 100 days.

The Masquerade

This potato has long been described as "edible art," and nothing comes closer to the truth. It is a unique potato, bicolor and marbled in brilliant yellow and purple and really has to be seen to be believed.

It is lower in starch than many varieties and has white, moist flesh ideal for mashing, baking, and roasting, and you only need to wait 63 days after planting to harvest these gorgeous potatoes.

The Princess Laratte

A popular potato in France, it is one of the superstars in European cuisine. It has a slightly sweet, nutty taste, and some have described it as a combination of almonds, hazelnuts, and chestnuts.

A slow variety to mature, the Laratte takes between 90 and 110 days to reach harvest time.

The Purple Majesty

For many people, yellow potatoes are the real ones, and many turn their noses up at anything different. However, purple potatoes not only look great, but they also taste great. Their skins are wine-dark, and the flesh is a succulent purple. A buttery, sweet spud, these are ideal for frying and for adding a real splash of color to your meal.

These potatoes love bright sunlight and take 85 days to mature into 3-to 4-inch long spuds.

The Swedish Peanut Fingerling

An heirloom variety, this fingerling has waxy flesh, firm and yellow with a wonderfully rich flavor. They are perfect for salads, roasting, and pan-frying.

Highly resistant to scab, this potato is a late-season one that matures in 90 days and produces 1 ½ inch long fingerlings.

The Yukon Gold

Everyone has heard of the Yukon Gold potato. Developed in the 1960s in Canada, it is a hybrid variety and a perfect all-rounder. Its waxiness ensures it holds its shape while boiling, but its fluffiness makes it great for mashing. It also roasts well, which is the most common use for the Yukon Gold. Roasted, it has creamy, buttery flesh with awesome crunchy skin.

It is an early potato, taking just 65 days to mature, and needs to be in full sun. It is a disease-resistant potato, including scab.

True Potato Seeds

While most people plant their potatoes using seed potatoes, some choose to use true seeds. Near the end of its life, the potato plant will produce berries, which are poisonous but contain seeds, known as TPS or True Potato Seeds. Not everyone will see these seed pods, mostly because of climate and cultivar. In fact, some people don't even see flowers on their plants, but it doesn't mean they aren't producing a harvest.

So, why do people choose to grow their potatoes from seed potatoes and not true seeds? That's where things get a little tricky. You see, the different varieties of potato you can grow are clones. Let's say you plant a Yukon Gold tuber. You are actually planting a part of the original plant grown back in the 1970s, and every generation is nothing more than another clone. These clones are somewhat predictable, and that's great for agriculture.

The true seed differs because it is the potato plant's progeny, and each one will differ from the next. Every seed from every single berry will produce a different potato plant – think of it as discovering new potato varieties with jumbled genetics. The potatoes you grow from seeds produced on your plants are unique to you and your garden. In effect, TPS means creating brand new varieties, and you can choose which ones to keep, based on what you want, even replanting the tubers for as long as you want.

Seed Potatoes vs. TPS

Seed Potatoes	True Potato Seeds
Seed tubers are genetically cloned from a parent plant	Seeds are plant progeny, each genetically unique
Produces uniform and predictable results	Produced diverse and unpredictable results
You can plant these straight into the soil	Like many other seeds, these need to be started indoors
Tubers are prone to diseases	Seeds rarely suffer or carry diseases
Tubers will last for around 12 months	Kept in the freezer, seeds will last for 50 years or more
A limited selection with no more than 100 varieties commercially available	A wide selection with almost unlimited and unusual types

Growing potatoes from true seeds are hit and miss – some may produce a fantastic yield, while others may produce nothing. On the whole, though, most will have a reasonable yield. Also, depending on the seeds you begin with, you may end up with all different colored potatoes, all shapes and sizes you won't see at the supermarket.

Seed potatoes are used in large-scale agriculture and are optimized to produce good yields in certain areas. If you are happy with the seed potatoes suited to your area, then TPS may not be for you – you are not likely to get any better traits than those already available. However, if the commercial spuds don't do well in your area or you just want to experiment, then have a go at TPS.

TPS opens the door to a new experience in terms of flavors, textures, and colors, and these can even be crossed with others to produce a new variety. It may seem intimidating, but we grow most vegetables from seed, so why not potatoes?

To get started, check your current plants for seed berries and save the ones you find. This doesn't always work because commercial seed potatoes rarely produce berries. You can, however, purchase seeds online and, when you've grown your first plants, save the berries from there.

They should be planted in pits, indoors, eight weeks before the last frost in your region; if possible, do it four weeks before so you don't get tempted to plant them too early. You will need some grow lights because the ambient indoor light is simply not enough, and the temperature should be between 50 and 70 degrees. Once your seedlings are around 6-inches tall, you can begin hardening them off before planting them outdoors – remember to bury them, leaving just the first set of leaves visible. From there, it's the same as growing seed potatoes.

How and Why to Chit Your Potatoes

In North America, many gardeners do not bother chitting their potatoes but simply plant them straight in the ground. However, chitting is one of the earliest garden terms and is something that has been practiced for a long time. There are so many reasons you should do it, but let's look first at what it is.

What is Potato Chitting?

Chitting is nothing more than allowing your potatoes to sprout under the right conditions before you plant them in the ground. This encourages shoots to come out from the potato, which should be hardy and strong, ensuring you plant only those potatoes that you know will grow. When you look at potatoes that have been kept in the dark or in supermarket shopping bags, their shoots are long, spindly, and white. This is because they are looking for light and will never be strong shoots. When you place a potato near the light, it need not search and can, instead, put out strong, short shoots.

Lots of people will tell you they have grown many a good crop without chitting their potatoes first, and sure, you can grow them without doing this. But you will more than likely find that while your top foliage is healthy and thick, there won't be so much growth going on under the ground.

Why You Should Chit Your Potatoes

There are three very good reasons you should chit your potatoes:

- It gives your potatoes a greater chance of growing successfully
- It speeds up the harvest time by about two weeks
- It gives you a much larger crop

In cooler regions, particularly in the north, the growing season is quite a bit shorter, and some gardeners feel like they are forever trying to beat the clock to get their harvests in. Failing to get the crops in time puts you at risk of frosts, which will damage and potentially kill off the harvest.

By taking the time to pre-sprout your potatoes, using warmer conditions and light, they get the strong shoots they need and, once you plant them, those shoots will just keep on growing. In short growing seasons, this is an effective method to ensure your crops are ready in time. If you don't chit the potatoes, they need an extra two or three weeks in the ground to start sending out the shoots, and those shoots may be too weak to sustain a decent harvest.

Chitting works well with early varieties, such as Purple Viking, Norland, Red Gold, Pacific Russet, Yukon Gold, and Purple Majesty.

Seed Potatoes vs. Store-Bought Potatoes

It's always best to start with seed potatoes as they are certified to be free of viruses and diseases. They are also developed specifically to produce much better, higher-yielding potatoes, and you get a great choice of varieties – earlies, second earlies, maincrops, and so on, plus heritage and heirlooms. By putting the money into the seed potatoes, you are guaranteed a healthy harvest that won't leave diseases or pathogens in the soil.

The potatoes you purchase in the store, on the other hand, are often sprayed with chemicals to slow down sprouting or stop it altogether. If you do get shoots from them, you won't know where they were grown and whether they are infected with soil-borne pathogens. Some pathogens will stay in your soil for many years and can have a detrimental effect on anything you plant there in the future.

Not only that, but you also don't always get a great selection of potatoes at the supermarkets. Most only carry a few varieties such as Yukon Gold, Russets, Red, White, and fingerling.

It really isn't worth risking your crop using potatoes that could potentially damage your soil and may not even produce a great harvest when seed potatoes are an inexpensive, safe way of growing.

How to Chit your Potatoes:

Chitting your potatoes is easy work, and the benefits are massive:

Tools

Here's what you will need:

- Your seed potatoes
- Egg cartons or a flat box with low sides
- Newspaper – if you are using a box
- A cool room with a window – room temperature must be above 50°F or 10°C

The Steps:

1. Start to chit your potatoes around six weeks before you intend to plant them.

2. Examine your seed potatoes carefully. Find the eyes as this is where the stems will grow – they look like small scars or nubs. Discard any that are moldy.

3. If there are any long stems, remove them. These sprouts are too weak and likely developed because there wasn't enough light. Cutting them off will cause much stronger shoots.

4. If you have large potatoes and they have several eyes on them, slice them, ensuring each piece has at least two eyes.

5. Stand the potatoes in an egg carton or a box with the eyes facing upward – if using a box, add a layer of newspaper first.

6. Set your boxes near the window in your cool room and leave them – check on them every couple of days to see if they are sprouting but do not let them freeze.

7. If you are planting more than one variety, label each box, so you know which potato is which.

Once your potatoes have produced good, healthy stems, plant them in the garden, in beds, or in containers.

Make sure the temperature is over 50°F/10°C – while potatoes can handle cool temperatures, they cannot take frost. If a late frost is forecasted, make sure you cover any foliage with a blanket or garden fleece or cover them with soil to protect them.

Before you plant them, ensure you remove all the stems bar the two or three strongest ones. If you have too many shoots, the seed potato will be too weak and cannot feed the rest of them.

If you cut your potatoes after chitting, leave them for a few days to dry before planting; otherwise, you risk the potato rotting.

Chapter 4: Cultivating Potatoes in Containers

If you have little space in your garden, have only a small terrace or a balcony, or cannot grow large amounts of crops in the ground, you can easily grow your potatoes in containers. This is also the ideal method for those with poor soil that isn't suited to the crop. It isn't just ideal for growing potatoes; you can grow just about any vegetable you want in containers, and while you may not get such a big harvest, with the right attention and growing conditions, you can still reap enough potatoes to keep you going.

Growing potatoes in containers is a little different from other vegetables. With most vegetable seeds or plants, you fill the container with soil and then bury the seedling or seed a few inches down. Root crops, like potatoes, grow much better if you plant them at the bottom of the container and then progressively add soil as the plant grows. That way, the potatoes have more room to produce more tubers.

Choosing Your Container

The possibilities are endless here. First off, you can buy potato bags. These are designed for root crops and can accommodate three or four seed potatoes, thus enhancing the chances of a great crop. Most of these bags have a window flap at the front where you can see the potatoes growing. These flaps also allow you to reach in and harvest just a few potatoes at a time without having to disturb the whole crop.

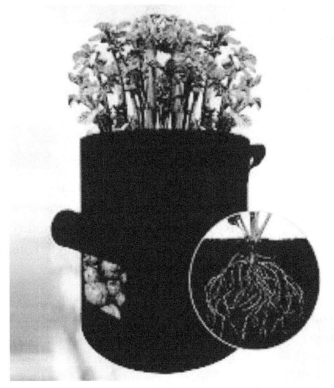

If your budget doesn't allow for these, or you want to use what you already have, any large container is suitable for planting potatoes in. You can use smaller ones, but you won't get so many potatoes in your harvest. Some people use dustbins - plastic ones are best - or water barrels. You can use ornamental plant containers, heavy burlap sacks, even stacks of tires. The burlap sacks provide great growing conditions because they are breathable, and water drains out quickly.

Whatever container you choose, remember that its size will affect how much you reap from the plant. If you choose smaller containers, you can grow only one plant per container, and you will need several to get the same yield as you do from larger containers like dustbins.

Really, it's up to you – pick whatever container suits your environment, budget, and what works in the space you have. All you need to ensure is that the container is clean and has drainage –you may make holes in the bottom of your container.

How Many Plants Per Container?

Again, that depends on the size of the container, but like any plant, over-planting will lead to a poor harvest, with small potatoes that are likely to be deformed – that's if they produce at all. Don't forget, each plant is fighting for the nutrients in the soil, and too many will simply fail to get enough for their needs. You need to consider that you should use 2.5 gallons (US) of soil (around 10 liters) per seed potato.

If you choose water barrels, dustbins, and other large containers, you can grow four plants comfortably, and that will require more soil and more watering. You can grow the same number of plants, one each in a smaller container, and use less soil.

A container approximately 1 ft. in diameter can take one plant. A 2 ft. container will take three, while the potato growing bags take three to four. In larger containers, four to five is possible.

There should be enough room in your container to add more soil as the plants grow. Otherwise, you won't get many tubers.

The Right Conditions for Potatoes In Containers

No matter what vegetables you grow in a container, you need to use good-quality soil. Your plants need healthy, rich, well-draining soil –the plants retain more food, and the soil retains more moisture than poor quality soil does.

Don't forget that your potatoes will need a decent amount of water. This is even more important when grown in containers because the soil will dry out much quicker. However, consistent watering will soon drain all the nutrients out of the soil, so ensure you add a high-quality, slow-release fertilizer when you plant your potatoes to ensure they stay fed. You can buy specific potato fertilizers, or you can use a product like *Blood, Fish, and Bone.*

You also need to ensure that the containers are placed where the temperature is a consistent 65-70°F. While they like full sun, too much direct sunlight can overheat potatoes in containers – this is more important if you live in southern regions with long hot summers. Ensure your potatoes can get some respite from the heat in this case.

One way to keep moisture in the soil in your containers is to add mulch when the soil reaches the top of the container. This also helps to shield the potatoes from sunlight – any exposed potatoes can turn green, and once this happens, they are bitter and not fit to eat.

Choosing the Right Variety

You can grow any variety of potatoes in a container and what you choose is down to what you want. Most container gardeners find that the first and second early varieties produce the best results as they tend to mature within 70 to 90 days.

Planting these also allows you to get your harvest in before the risk of summer blight. Some varieties that work well are Nicola, Swift, Charlotte, Anya, Lady Christi, or Rocket.

Whatever you go for, purchase disease-free seed potatoes.

Now onto the good bit – getting your hands dirty!

How to Grow Potatoes in Containers

Here's what you need to grow your potatoes in containers:

- A garden trowel
- A container
- Seed potatoes
- Soil
- Fertilizer

Instructions

Step One – Prepare the Soil

Have high-quality soil that drains well. Try to choose organic where you can.

Step Two – Add Some Fertilizer

You need to add organic fertilizer, preferably slow-release. Mix it into the soil well, ensuring it is distributed throughout. On top of this, every couple of weeks, a diluted liquid fertilizer should be applied to the plants. The constant watering of the plants will leach the nutrients out, and those need to be replaced often.

Using organic fertilizers is best – if you accidentally use a little too much, it won't matter, whereas using too much commercial fertilizer can burn the plants.

Step Three – Preparing the Seed Potatoes

If you have been carefully reading this chapter, you will already know the benefits of chitting your potatoes, and the process is the same for growing in containers. If you haven't done so, follow the instructions from the last chapter to chit your potatoes to get them ready for planting.

Step Four – Planting the Potatoes

Put your container in a sunny position and add four to six inches of your prepared soil. Position the seed potatoes on the soil, making sure the eyes face upward. Leave enough room between each potato as they need room to grow. For example, in a 20-inch diameter container, you can place about four potatoes. It might look like a lot, but you will be pleasantly surprised when it comes time to pull in the harvest.

Step Five – Cover Your Potatoes

Add two inches of your soil over the top of the potatoes – no more than four inches as the potatoes will grow quickly. A rule of thumb – the warmer your climate is, the more soil you need.

Step Six – Tend Your Crops

Potatoes require sun and water to grow, so make sure your container is positioned where it can receive between six and eight hours of sun per day, as a minimum. Water them well but don't flood them. Too much water will only rot the potatoes and destroy any chance of a harvest.

Check on your containers at least once a day. Check the moisture levels in one of two ways – stick your finger into the soil, about an inch - if it feels dry, water the potatoes. In hot, windy conditions, your containers may need watering more than once a day. The other option is to purchases a moisture meter – you can get these online or at your local garden center.

When you water your containers, do it deeply. When you see water running out of the bottom of the container, you know it's been watered well. Only watering the top surface is not enough.

Step Seven – Hill Your Potatoes

When your plants are about six inches tall, they need to be hilled. This means you need to add more of your prepared soil around the plants, covering the stems and being careful not to break them. You want to bury about a third of the plant, leaving just the top leaves uncovered. What you bury will produce even more potatoes, so this is a critical process for getting a good harvest.

This process must be repeated until the soil fills your container. Potatoes are fast-growing plants, so monitor them carefully.

Step Eight – Harvest Time!

Once your plants have flowered, you can begin harvesting.

Reach into the soil and pull a few tubers out carefully. These are perfect for new potatoes and can be harvested a few at a time – the remaining potatoes will simply continue growing. Later on, when the plant has died back, the rest of the potatoes can be harvested. Lay a tarpaulin on the ground or have a clean wheelbarrow to tip the container into it. Then, you can simply go through the soil and remove all the potatoes.

If you see small ones, don't be tempted to throw them away – these are wonderfully sweet and perfect in a stew.

If you see any green potatoes, throw them away. The green ones contain a chemical called solanine, and it is bitter, slightly toxic, and may cause issues with your digestive system.

Pros and Cons of Growing Potatoes in Containers

As with anything, using containers to grow your potatoes comes with its own set of pros and cons.

Pros

- You get more flexibility than with other methods. You don't need large amounts of land, and you can grow in just about any size or type of container you want.

- Ideal for those who cannot physically handle the work involved in growing potatoes the traditional way. Container gardening is popular now, and containers can be lifted to a height to suit the person, which means those who physically cannot bend or get down low enough to tend to their plants can still grow their own spuds.

- Growing in containers means you can have them right outside your door or on your patio for easy access and quick harvesting.

- Containers are much easier to maintain because you are less likely to suffer from weeds and pests. Any weeds that do grow are simple to pull out. This method can also help you manage potato pests as, depending on where you place your containers, they are less likely to be overcome with slugs, snails, and other crawling pests.

- Containers can be moved where you want them, which means you can move them to take full advantage of the best growing conditions, following the sun around during the day. To help with this, you can stand your containers on wheeled stands.

Cons

• To get a decent crop, you need very large containers or lots of smaller ones. Plus, the only way you can take advantage of companion planting is to use yet more containers as you can't plant anything else with the potatoes.

• The containers need to be reasonably deep for a successful crop.

• You may find yourself watering more as containers don't hold the same amount of water in the soil as raised beds or ground beds do. In hot conditions, you may find yourself watering up to three times a day.

In a later chapter, we will discuss how to store your potato crop.

Chapter 5: Cultivating Potatoes in Raised Beds

Raised bed gardens provide one of the most efficient and productive ways of growing food. You have much more control over the soil, and you can quickly harvest your crops. The type of raised bed you use depends entirely on what you want - you can build a simple square or rectangle from wood, or you can be more elaborate.

How to Build Raised Beds

Building your own raised bed garden is a great project for those who intend to grow a lot of their own food since most vegetables will grow quite easily in them. All you need is some tools and hard work.

Step One - Choose your location

The location is most important because you are unlikely to move it anywhere once your bed is built. So, it must be placed in full sun as all vegetables need plenty of sunlight to grow. Try to build it on level ground if you can - it will be so much easier. And last, unless you want them on full show, vegetable beds can be tucked in between other beds, so they don't detract from everything else in the garden when the season is done.

Step Two – Choose your material

You can build raised beds from just about any material but the most commonly used in rot-resistant wood that has NOT been treated. Do not use railway ties if you can avoid it – these have been treated with creosote. Wood treatments tend to leak toxins into the soil over time, which will have a detrimental effect on your plants.

Other options include:

- **Stacked Stone Raised Beds**

Stacked stones make great raised beds, although they are more expensive (unless you have the stone lying around – and take longer to build than traditional wooden ones. They do, however, look good in the garden.

- Recycled Redwood Raised Beds

Recycled redwood beds are a more eco-friendly choice, and redwood is far less prone to rotting than other woods.

- Woven Wattle Raised Beds

You can build woven wattle beds in any shape you want, although circular beds are easier to build. Twigs are woven together in the same baskets are made, and you can even add canes or trellises to create a tepee shape to grow other plants on layered shelves.

• **Redwood Box Raised Planters**

Redwood planters are easy to make and ideal for those who don't have a great deal of space available. These are smaller, self-contained beds that are easy to control and harvest, and you can even move them to different locations if you want.

Step Three – Work out how large you want the bed and how you want it laid out

Next, determine the size and shape of your plant bed. Most people stick to square,

Or rectangular beds.

But you can have any shape you want, including this lovely pentagon shape.

An L-shaped bed:

Or even a walk-in raised bed, like this:

Regardless of the shape and size, there are some general rules to follow. First, your beds should never be over four feet wide. This size makes it easy to reach the center from any side. Second, they should be between 12 and 24 inches deep and, third, if you have more than one bed, try to leave at least 18 inches between them as a pathway. That way, you can walk between them and get your wheelbarrow down there when it's time to bring in your harvest.

Step Four - Time to build your beds

For this, we'll assume you are building a standard square or rectangular bed from wood.

1. Measure your planks and cut them to the length you want.

2. Use galvanized screws or brackets to hold the corners together. Some people also used wooden corner posts to give the bed a bit more stability.

If you choose to use stone, you can stack them together without needing any mortar to hold them.

Step Five – Line your beds

You don't have to do this if you don't want to, but lining your beds with cardboard, newspaper, or weed suppressant material will prevent your beds from becoming overrun with grass and weeds from the underlying soil.

Step Six – Fill your beds with soil

Use a good compost soil for this, or, to make your own mix, use equal parts of well-mixed manure, topsoil, and sand. There are plenty of ready-bagged soils available in garden centers too. Mix a handful of slow-release granular fertilizer evenly into the soil. You can purchase potato fertilizer or use an all-purpose one like Blood, Fish, and Bone.

Step Seven – Plant your potatoes

Because you have used fresh soil, digging your potatoes in will be easy. Dig evenly spaced trenches along the length of your beds, digging as deep as you can without disturbing the bottom layer. Leave 18 inches between rows if you can.

Place the potatoes, eyes up, about a foot apart, then cover them with soil. You can also layer mulch over the top at this stage, using grass clipping, straw, dead, crumbled leaves, or pine needles. As the plants grow, add more mulch or soil to keep most of the plant covered until you get to the top of the bed. This ensures more tubers can grow in the root system.

Watering Your Raised Beds

Potatoes need quite a lot of water, and the best way to know when to water them is to feel the soil. If it's dry, give them a drink. Potatoes do not like wet soggy soil any more than they do dry soil, so deep water them once a week, more if your weather is particularly hot. The best time to water is first thing in the morning or in the evening, before and after the hottest part of the day.

Some gardeners prefer to hand water their beds, partly because they love to be in the garden and partly because they can keep an eye on their plants. Some even find it therapeutic. You can use a hose pipe or a watering can - it will all depend on how you want to do it. You can also attach a watering wand to your hose pipe - these spread further and allow you to get water quickly to all of your plants.

An alternative method is an automatic irrigation system. Not everyone has time to stand and water their beds, so you can use drip irrigation or soaker hoses. The latter work by allowing water to seep out of the entire length of the hose - simply lay the hose around the bed and plug it in. The water will reach deep down to the roots where it is needed, and you can leave it to do its work while you get on with something else. Drip irrigation works by sending water straight to the roots from emitters. If it's ease you want, soaker hoses are the best bet.

Choosing Your Potatoes

The best types of potatoes for raised beds are the early varieties because they are quicker to mature, and the entire crop comes at the same time. Usually, these mature within 65 to 80 days of planting or, if you want small, new potatoes, start harvesting just after flowering. Some of the best varieties are Dark Red Norland, Yukon Gold, Red Gold, Sangre, Chieftain, and Irish Cobbler.

Fingerling potatoes are also suited to raised beds. These are small, narrow potatoes, about 2 to 4 inches long. They come in many colors like red, purple, orange, and white, with the flesh being the same colors. They have a nutty, mild taste, somewhat earthy, and a moist, firm texture. Some of the best varieties are Banana, AmaRosa, Rose Finn Apple, Pinto, and French Fingerling.

Pros and Cons of Growing Potatoes in Raised Beds

All vegetable growing methods have their own ups and downs, and growing potatoes in raised beds come with their own set.

Pros

- You can harvest high yields of potatoes, given that the plant has more room to spread its roots and produce tubers.
- Raised beds tend to have better drainage, ensuring your potatoes won't rot.
- Raised beds are easier for planting as you can build them, so you need not crawl around on the ground or bend down to plant and tend to your potatoes.
- You can control the soil and water conditions in the bed, where it is more difficult in the ground.

Cons

- You need to build the beds first, and this can be labor-intensive. You can purchase prefab beds you just put together, but the cost may put some people off.
- Harvesting may be tricky. If the sides of your beds don't come off, you will need to dig the potatoes out.
- Raised beds often need more water than in-ground growing.

Chapter 6: Cultivating Potatoes in Bags

If you have a large garden and plenty of space, or access to a good-sized allotment, you can increase the size of your crop by growing your potatoes in the ground. But not everyone is blessed with the space to do this, and some simply don't want the work involved. That's where potato bags come in. We mentioned these earlier in the section on containers, but this is a little more in-depth.

What Are Potato Grow Bags?

You can buy specific bags online or from a garden center, or you can make your own. The bags you purchase can be made from plastic or felt, and some even have windows in the front which allow you to see what's going on in your potato bag and let you harvest a few potatoes at a time without disturbing the entire crop.

However, you can just as easily make your own from burlap, weed suppressant fabric, and so on. Growing in bags is the same as containers – the soil is layered up over the potatoes as they grow, giving them room to produce more tubers. When you cover the root zone on a seed potato, it encourages more roots to grow. Using bags allows you to control the conditions your potatoes are grown in and makes them much easier to harvest.

Making Your Own Grow Bags

Simply get some old burlap sacks – these are very strong and breathable – and roll the tops down. You can also sew some weed suppressant fabric together (or staple it), leaving enough at the top to unroll as you layer on the soil. Alternatively, if you have large bags of compost, cut the top off one and empty the soil out, leaving just a few inches in the bottom. Roll the top down and plant your potatoes.

The Best Potatoes for Bags

Before you plant your potatoes, determine which ones you want. As a recap, there are three main types of potatoes you can grow:

- **First earlies** – Fastest to grow, typically what we consider to be new potatoes.

- **Second earlies** – Also new potatoes but take longer to grow.

- **Maincrops** – Take longer to mature but produce the best potatoes for mashing, roasting, and baking. Typically, these are ready to harvest from late July through September.

Most gardeners plant first and second earlies in bags, leaving the maincrop potatoes to grow in the ground.

When To Plant in Bags?

Traditionally, most gardeners plant potatoes in March, but it will depend on the variety you choose. If you choose the first earlies, you can grow them in April and May as well, ensuring you get a supply of potatoes throughout the summer months.

How Long Do Potatoes Take to Grow In Bags?

Again, this depends on the type of potato you choose to grow, along with the weather:

- **First Early** – take about ten weeks to mature after planting
- **Second Early** – take about 13 weeks to mature after planting
- **Maincrop** – take about 20 weeks to mature after planting

Decide when you want your potatoes, and that will determine the variety of potatoes you grow. If you plant in March, April or May, select first and second earlies.

Now you are ready to buy your potatoes.

As you now know, seed potatoes are specifically developed and grown to make it easier for you to grow your own crop of potatoes and are certified as free of viruses and disease. While you can plant them straight into the soil and hope for the best, you get a much better chance of success if you pre-sprout or chit your potatoes first. Again, as a recap, simply place your seed potatoes in an egg carton or low-sided cardboard box and leave them somewhere light, airy, and cool. Sprouts will appear from the potato eyes and should be strong and green, which can save you two to three weeks of waiting when you plant the potatoes in the bags.

How to Plant Your Potato Bags

There are two ways to do this – the traditional way or the modern way.

Traditional Method

1. Layer a couple of inches of compost in the bottom of the bag.

2. Lay your potatoes – no more than three or four – on the soil, sprouts facing upward.

3. Cover the potatoes with soil and water – fertilizer can also be added to the soil beforehand.

4. As your potatoes grow, layer more soil on, covering two-thirds of the plant.

5. Continue in this manner, ensuring your potatoes are kept watered until the soil fills the bag.

The Modern Method

Hilling is no longer considered necessary, especially where potatoes are grown in bags, so long as you protect your potatoes from the sunlight using the soil and the plant foliage:

1. Use an 8-liter potato bag and fill it with good compost to about an inch below the top.

2. Plunge one chitted potato, sprouts upward, into the center of the compost, about 5 inches down.

3. Cover it with soil and water.

4. Leave the bag somewhere warm and bright, where it cannot be affected by frost and water regularly.

5. Once the foliage begins to show, feed the plant every two weeks with fertilizer and water when the bagged soil looks like it is drying out.

When to Harvest Your Potatoes

When you harvest your potatoes will depend on the variety you have planted and the size of potato you want. If you want new potatoes, plant first earlies and harvest them as soon as the flowers begin showing – this should be about ten weeks after planting.

If you planted maincrop potatoes, leave the stems and leaves to wither before you cut them down. Now you should leave the potatoes in the ground for a further two weeks before you harvest them, giving the potato skins time to set. If you spot any signs of blight on your potato foliage, cut it down and destroy it straight away, preferably by burning.

If you plant second-cropping potatoes, commonly called Christmas potatoes, these can usually be harvested from the end of November onwards – they can be left in the soil until you are ready to use them. When the leaves wither and go yellow, they should be cut back. Then cover the soil in the bag with a thick straw layer or move them into a greenhouse, a polytunnel, or indoors.

To discover if your potatoes are ready to harvest, dig gently in the soil and see how big they are. If they are still too small, leave them a bit longer.

Pros and Cons of Growing Potatoes in Bags

Now you know how to grow your potatoes in bags, time to finish with the pros and cons of this method:

Pros

- You need little land. In fact, you can grow them on balconies if you live in an apartment or small house with little to no garden.

- This is an environmentally sound way of growing potatoes as it conserves the soil, stopping it from being degraded.

- You can get the maximum productivity from a few bags, offering high yields.

- It is far less labor-intensive than other methods.

- Using the right sacks means you can keep the moisture in the soil for longer, thus, less watering.

- It is far easier to control pests and diseases.

Cons

- You may not get the potatoes you want as earlies tend to sell out quickly.

- You must monitor your water, fertilizer, pesticide, insecticide, and other inputs vigilantly.

- Be sure you can keep your bags at the right temperatures – too hot, and the potatoes won't germinate and develop properly, too cold, and the plants may die.

- Bag-grown potatoes don't always have such a large root system, so you need to ensure that the bottom layer of soil is very fertile and rich.

Chapter 7: Growing Potatoes in the Ground

If you have a large garden and are happy to spend the time, you can grow a great crop of potatoes right in the ground. And you can start early once the soil is workable and has no frost left in it.

When to Plant Your Potatoes

There is plenty of folklore about the best time to plant potatoes in the garden. New England old-timers used to plant theirs when they saw dandelions starting to bloom in the open fields. The Pennsylvania Dutch waited until March 17th – St. Patrick's Day or, as it was known then, St. Gertrude's Day, while many Christians chose Good Friday as they believed that was the day the devil had no power over them.

Whenever you plant yours, remember that potatoes like cooler weather. In the Northern regions, gardeners opt to plant their first crop of earlies early to mid-April, roughly six to eight weeks before the last frost or once the soil is workable. While potatoes like cool weather, it's a very fine line to determine because they don't like frost. If the forecast indicates that night-time temperatures will drop below freezing once your potatoes are in the ground, cover them, especially if there is foliage showing. Use plastic sheets, containers, or anything else, as long as you remember to take the cover off in the morning. Here's a couple of tips to help you:

- Try to avoid frosts by starting your planting up to two weeks after the last spring frost. Earlier is okay if you remember that frost can damage potatoes or cause the soil to become too wet.

- Don't go by the calendar to plant your crops – use the soil to tell you. The ideal soil temperature should be at least 50°F or 10°C. It should also not be soaking wet, so much so it clumps and can't easily be worked – if you have had a lot of rain, leave your soil to drain through a bit first. Plant potatoes on soggy ground, and they will rot.

You can grow potatoes as winter crops in the southern regions, planting any time between September and February - if your winters are mild, plant in September. Central Florida farmers start planting in January, while Georgian farmers start in February.

What you grow is also a consideration. First and second earlies are the most popular and the most expensive to purchase from the supermarkets, which is why many people opt to grow their own – that and the fact that they taste so much better, of course. These crops tend to take less growing room and are not so susceptible to blight since they are harvested earlier than maincrops.

The maincrops take much longer to mature and require more space between plants. They are also more prone to blight, so more attention is needed. Maincrop potatoes are more suitable for storage too.

Here's a guide on when to plant and harvest earlies and maincrop:

• First Early

Otherwise known as new potatoes, these are planted in March, with frost protection if needed, and harvested in June through July. They should be planted 30 cm apart, about 12 cm deep, and each row should be 60 cm apart.

The best varieties are Lady Christyl (shown below), Rocket, Orla, and Red Duke of York.

• Second Early

These take about 14 to 16 weeks to come to maturity. They can be planted in March with frost protection, if needed, and harvested between July and August. Plant them 30 cm apart, 12 cm down, and each row should be 60 cm apart.

The best varieties are Ratte, Maris Piper (shown below), and Charlotte.

- Maincrop

These will take between 16 and 22 weeks to mature and can be planted from mid to late April, harvesting between August and October. They should be planted 40 cm apart, 12 cm deep, and the rows should be 75 cm apart.

The best varieties are Desiree, Pink Fir Apple (shown below), Sarpo Mira, King Edward, Cara, and Maris Piper.

- Salad Potatoes

Salad or new potatoes are waxy and firm, with a sweet, almost nutty flavor. These are first or second earlies and should be harvested when the flowers begin showing on the plants.

Preparing the Ground

Before you can even think about growing your potatoes, you need to do some groundwork – quite literally. Choose where you want to grow your potatoes well in advance of your planting day, preferably in November of the previous year. The site needs to be thoroughly weeded, removing all the roots, and thoroughly dug over. Any large stones in the ground should be removed, and lots of high-potash fertilizer and well-rotted organic manure should be dug in.

Try to choose somewhere with full sun and an open position with well-drained, fertile soil. Do not plant potatoes in the same place two years running as the first year's crop will deplete the soil of many nutrients, and you also risk soil-borne diseases.

Potatoes like slightly acidic soil. If your soil is alkaline, you can place a line of sulfur across the top of the ridge after you plant your potatoes. This will ensure the maximum yield and deter scab and other skin blemish issues common to alkaline soil.

Chitting

Seed potatoes like to be chitted as it gives them a good head start with strong shoots. Between late January and early February, place your seed potatoes in egg cartons or a cardboard box in a light, cool, frost-free room. Once you see shoots start to form, leave them until they are about an inch long and they are ready to plant. If you have several shoots, you can do one of two things – remove all but the strongest few or cut the potatoes, ensuring each piece has a couple of strong shoots. If you do cut them, they must dry out for a few days. Otherwise, they may rot.

Planting Your Potatoes

Refer to the table below to determine planting times for your potatoes, taking soil conditions and the weather into account at the same time.

Crop	Planting Time	Planting Distance Rows	Distance Between Rows	Harvest Time – Approx.
First Early	End of Feb onwards	30 cm apart	60 cm apart	After 10 weeks
Second Early	Mid-March onwards	37 cm apart	75 cm apart	After 13 weeks
Early Maincrop	From late March	45 cm	75 cm	After 15 weeks
Maincrop	From late March	45 cm	75 cm	After 20 weeks
Second Cropping	Early August	30 cm	60 cm	After 11 weeks

Time to plant

Step One

Use a shovel with a round point or a hoe and dig trenches around six inches wide and eight inches deep. They should taper to about 3 inches at the bottom.

Step Two

Add well-rotted manure, organic compost, or if you grow Comfrey in your garden, line the trench with fresh Comfrey leaves.

Step Three

Place your potatoes the recommended distance apart in the trench with the sprouts pointing upward. Hose the soil back over the top to a depth of about three to four inches.

Between 12 and 16 days, after you plant your potatoes, you should start to see sprouts appear. Gently hoe another three or four inches of soil over the top, leaving the tip of the plant uncovered. Repeat this a few weeks later, ensuring a hill of about four or five inches of soil above ground level.

Also, once you see the potato plants appear, place an organic mulch between the rows. This will preserve moisture in the soil and keep the soil cooler, which will help keep the weeds down.

More About Hilling

Hilling is a critical part of growing potatoes as it stops the tubers from being exposed to sunlight and turning green (and poisonous). It is a simple process.

As the potato plant grows, the main stem is produced above the ground; this has the leaves, and eventually, the flowers on it. Beneath the ground is where a lot more work is going on. Secondary stems are produced below the surface of the soil, which is where the tubers form. To stop the shallow ones from being exposed to the sun, hill up the soil around the plant, which also encourages more tubers to grow. This is done about three or four times during a growing season.

Some tips to help you:

• Hill your potatoes first thing in the morning, which is when your plants are tallest as, throughout the heat of the day, they will begin to droop.

• Ensure even moisture is maintained from the sprout's first appearance until a month or two after they flower. Each potato plant will require between one and two inches of water per week, a little less in cooler periods and a bit more in the hotter periods. If you give them too much water right after you plant them and not enough when the tubers have begun forming, you will end up with small and misshapen potatoes.

• The final hilling is done just before the flowers appear – the plant above the ground will be about a foot tall. Hill the dirt up around the base, ensuring the tubers are covered and the plant is supported.

As a last piece of advice, if you do not get sufficient rain, make sure your potatoes are watered regularly, especially while the tubers develop.

Harvesting Your Potatoes

Harvesting depends on several things – the variety you planted, weather conditions, and what size potatoes you want. The longer you leave your potatoes in the ground, the bigger they will grow so, if you want nice small ones, start harvesting when your potato plants begin flowering, around ten weeks after you planted them.

If you plant maincrops, they fare best if you leave them in the ground for two more weeks after the plants have died back. This allows the skins to set. As your plants begin withering and turning yellow, cut the stems back to just above the soil level. Also do this if you spot blight on any plant.

Second-Cropping

If you grow second-cropping potatoes, plant them in August, earlier rather than later. These potatoes need not be chitted as they will do this themselves just after you plant them. Around 10 to 11 weeks after you plant the potatoes, you should be able to harvest tubers about the size of a ping pong ball. Cut the stems back to just above the soil level, and then you can harvest as and when you want the potatoes.

Use sacking or thick straw layers to protect your potatoes from early frosts and, although you may have to battle wireworm and slugs, you should be able to dig potatoes right up to Christmas.

Once you have harvested them, lay them on the soil surface and leave them for a couple of hours. This dries the skin and cures it so you can store the potatoes, which we will discuss in a later chapter.

Pros and Cons

While many gardeners choose this method of growing potatoes, it too has its own set of pros and cons.

Pros

- You can get a much larger harvest of potatoes, both early and main crops.
- You have a much wider choice of varieties, given that ground-growing suits all types of potato.
- You can have several varieties growing at the same time.

Cons

- Potatoes grown in the ground require deep watering at least once per week, around an inch or so of water each time. This can be time-consuming if you grow large amounts unless you choose a soaker or drip-hose irrigation system.
- Planting potatoes in the ground is far more labor-intensive – the ground must be prepared weeks beforehand, and trenches need to be dug. Plus, you may have many more potatoes to hill up every few weeks.
- Outdoor potatoes tend to attract more pests and diseases and can be harder to monitor.

Chapter 8: Growing Potatoes in Mulch

Potatoes are one of the top crops grown by gardeners at home and are one of the first things that new gardeners try. However, digging potatoes out of the ground is not so popular these days, especially for those with bad backs or other complaints that make digging difficult. That's where the no-dig method comes in.

Pros and Cons

No-dig potatoes are grown beneath a thick layer of mulch, most commonly straw, and there are several reasons it is so popular

- When you grow your potatoes in straw or other mulch, they are less likely to be blemished than those grown under the soil.
- Straw helps keep the soil temperature down.
- Weeds don't tend to be so much of a problem.
- The tubers are less likely to be attacked by diseases or pests.
- No digging means less waste because potatoes are not stabbed by forks or sliced by spades.
- The mulch breaks down, feeding and nourishing your soil.
- You need not water so much as the mulch cools the soil and helps retain moisture.

Cons

However, like all potato growing methods, the no-dig method also has its downsides:

- Mulch doesn't protect from late-season frost, so those who plant their potatoes too early in mulch are risking losing their crop.
- Potatoes take up to two weeks longer to start growing than those planted in soil.
- Your crops are more susceptible to pests that attack above the ground.
- You may not get such a large crop.

Preparing Your Potato Bed

First, get your potatoes prepared; small ones are ideal or larger ones cut into two-inch pieces. Only use seed potatoes that are certified as disease-free and make sure each piece has at least one eye. Leave cut potatoes to dry for a day or two.

Before your potatoes are planted, treat the soil with fertilizer and weed control, preferably safe and organic mixtures. You can also add compost into the soil to add some nourishment. Break the soil up, remove any large weeds, and loosen all the soil to allow aeration and drainage.

Planting Your Potatoes

Step One

Thoroughly hoe the soil where your potatoes will grow. While the mulch will kill off most weeds, hoeing ensures the soil is loose. After, add a layer of compost over the soil and give the area a good watering.

Step Two

Place your potatoes on the soil's surface. Space them the same way as if you were planting them in the soil or in a bed. For a bed layout, space the potatoes 35 to 40 cm apart in all directions for early varieties, while a row layout would be 30 cm between potatoes and 45 to 50 cm between rows. For maincrop varieties, plant them 45 cm apart in all directions for a bed layout, or for a ground layout, plant them 35 cm apart with 75 cm between the rows.

Step Three

Now is the time to cover your potatoes. Most gardeners choose straw, but you can use woodchips or leaves if you prefer. You can also layer compost over the potatoes before you add your mulch. How thick your layer is depends on the work you want to put in – you can either start with a thin layer and build it up (the no-dig version of hilling) or dump a several-inch thick layer of straw or mulch on straight away.

Step Four

Water the mulch well. When you grow potatoes in this way, the mulch dries out quicker than the soil, so getting off to a good start with sufficiently moist mulch is the best way to ensure a healthy crop.

Step Five

Tether your mulch – otherwise, the wind will quite happily scatter it all over your garden! Use fleece, a wire mesh, or even a thick layer of fresh grass cuttings for this – you will see when the plants are ready to start pushing their way through. When the plants begin to show, you can remove the cover and, if the mulch is holding some sprouts back from getting through, give them a helping hand. From here on, you can add more straw, but many gardeners choose layers of grass clippings. Grass mats together, stopping the wind from taking it and a good layer keeps the light away from the tubers. Be careful, though – if you are using fresh clippings, don't heap them up against the stems. Grass is slightly acidic and, as it decomposes, it produces heat which can damage your potatoes plants.

From here on, simply top up the mulch when needed and water as required. When it comes to harvest time, the no-dig method comes into its own. You need not disturb the entire plant to get a few potatoes – just move the mulch aside carefully. If your potatoes aren't large enough, replace the mulch and leave them to grow a little longer.

Maintaining Your Crop

Planting the potatoes is just the first step. Maintaining them is important so, every now and then, look for weeds and remove them as soon as they appear. While you won't see many when you grow in this way, but the odd one may push its way through.

Ensure you keep the mulch moist, not soaking wet. If it's too wet, the potatoes will rot, but moist mulch can provide a continuous supply of water without drowning them.

Once you see the shoots coming through the mulch, remove whatever you tethered the mulch down with to allow the shoots to grow. From here on, you can use grass clippings.

When the shoots are a few inches above the surface, mound more hay around them to stop the tubers from becoming exposed. Keep watering and using fertilizer every couple of weeks.

Harvest Time

If you want early potatoes, wait until your plants begin flowering. While they are not fully mature, the potatoes are fine to eat – simply move the mulch aside to harvest what you want. Alternatively, leave the plants until the vines have died back – the potatoes are fully mature. You don't have to harvest the whole plant either; simply pull a few off and leave the rest to continue growing.

Chapter 9: Practical Tips on Caring for Your Potato Plants

Potatoes really are an easy crop to grow. So much so that if you just shoved a couple of seed potatoes in the ground and left them to their own devices, you would get something from them. However, they will reward you with a great crop of tasty spuds with a little care and attention.

Their first requirement is water, more so when they are young and have only shallow roots. A lack of water means the tubers won't form properly, and you are headed for a poor crop. Second, they need feeding and weeding. Potatoes are continuously hungry and need nitrogen, and weeds simply take all the goodness out of the soil. Last, they also need to be protected from late frosts.

Earthing Up

Also called "hilling," earthing up needs to happen a few times throughout the growing season. It isn't difficult; you have only to draw the soil up, using a hoe or your hands, about 10 cm on either side of the rows and pile it up against the potato plants.

This has a few benefits:

- The potato tubers growing near the soil surface are given an extra cover of soil. This stops them from being exposed to the light and going green. If you eat green potatoes, you risk severe stomach cramps, among other issues.

- Earthing up also loosens the soil, giving the tubers more room to form and grow.

- As you earth up, you can remove weeds, eliminating competition for the soil's nutrients.

The first time you do this should be when your plants are around 10 cm tall. Cover the first set of leaves on the plant with the soil. Do not compact it down; just pat it gently around the plants.

Do it again around four weeks later.

If you plant your potatoes approximately 60 to 75 cm apart, as is the recommended spacing, you might find it troublesome to earth up your plants. When you remove soil from between the plants to earth up, you are likely to do one of two things – dig up smaller potatoes growing away from the main plant or expose tubers to the light.

You can get around this in two ways. First, put a greater distance between the rows, between 90 and 100 cm. This gives you room to earth up without upsetting the plants and potatoes growing near the surface.

The second step is to add a three-inch deep layer of mulch between the rows. Use whatever you have – straw, wood chips, leaves, grass clippings, etc. You can even use well-rotted manure or compost.

When you harvest your potatoes, you can dig the mulch back into the soil, thus putting back the nutrients the potatoes took out and feeding the ground to be ready for next year.

Potatoes and Frost

Potatoes do prefer cooler weather, but late frosts can do an awful lot of damage, especially if your potato plant is now growing above the surface. If late frosts are threatening your crops, there are two things you can do. First, use straw or fleece to cover your plants to keep the frost off. Second, earth up early but, this time, cover the entire plant. Don't worry – your plants will soon come through the soil again.

If your potatoes do get caught with a late frost, don't worry too much. Provided the frost wasn't a severe one, your plants will recover throughout the growing cycle. If any of the stems are badly damaged, clip them off. The rest of the foliage will recover and will likely produce a decent crop.

Feeding Your Potatoes

Provided you feed your potato plants sufficiently, they will thrive. The leafy part of the plant above the ground needs nitrogen, and a small amount of this comes from the well-rotted compost you should have dug into the ground the year before. You can use nitrogen feed bought from the garden store as well, although it will wash out eventually as the plants are watered. This is the feed to give your plants for the first six or eight weeks while they are developing.

Later, as the tubers start forming, the plants will require potash to help the potatoes form; this is especially important for maincrops where you want the larger potatoes for storage.

Feeding with potash can be done in many ways, and one of the easiest is to use a liquid tomato feed – do follow the instructions on the pack to apply it. Eventually, the potash will be watered right down to the potato roots.

Another way is to use burned pruning, or if you have a wood-burning stove, use the ash from that. This should be scattered over the soil and lightly worked in using a trowel - rain will do the rest of the work.

There is a warning that goes with using ash - you must be certain of the wood source. If you burn old furniture or treated wood, the ash will have harmful chemicals in it. You also shouldn't use ash from a fire where other things have been burned alongside the wood.

If you dug in manure or compost the year before, use something like Blood, Fish, and Bone or Bonemeal fertilizer. These are slow-release fertilizers that last a long time and should be spread at a rate of a handful per square meter.

If you didn't add the compost, use the long-lasting fertilizers but add fast-acting fertilizer as well, using the same rate of spreading.

Watering Your Potatoes

When your plants are young, they need regular watering to help the tubers form – aim for a deep watering once per week, about an inch of water per plant at a time.

Once your potato plants are fully established, they need little water. When you earth them up, the soil keeps moisture in, helping water your tubers. Plus, a fully mature plant has a good root system that digs down for moisture.

If you live in a very dry area and you try to water your plants, you will need large volumes of water to get to the lower roots. If you only water enough to wet the surface, then you are encouraging the roots to grow close to the surface, not good if you want the roots to dig down for deeper water supplies. If you do need to water your potatoes, you are better off using a soaker hose. This not only directs the water straight down to the roots, but it also uses far less water, and you can leave it to run while you do other things – don't forget you leave it running, though!

Other Potato Care

Your potato plants will require weeding until they get to about 30 cm in height. After that, earthing up should take care of any other weeds that grow. If you allow too many weeds to grow at an early stage, they will take all the nutrients and water out of the soil, leaving your potatoes fighting for survival.

Potatoes produce flowers, and some may even go on to produce seeds. Do not remove the flowers – they tell you when your potatoes are growing and are an indicator of when you can harvest new potatoes.

Usually, the flowers will dry up and fall off, but some plants will produce berries. These contain the true potato seeds and, while they are not harmful to the plant, they do contain high levels of solanine, the same toxin found in green potatoes. For that reason, they must not be consumed. If your flowers do turn to berries, remove them immediately. While they don't harm the plant, they can stop the plant from directing energy into growing tubers.

You can harvest the berries and store the seeds inside for the following year – see the chapter on true potato seeds for more information. However, for beginners, this isn't a recommended route to take – it is far easier just to buy certified seed potatoes.

Companion Planting

Companion planting is a tried and tested method of keeping diseases and pests away from plants, and while some plants are great in helping potatoes grow, some cause problems. When planting potatoes, keep the following in mind:

- Tomatoes, squash, cucumber, pumpkin, and raspberries are more likely to develop blight if you plant them near potatoes.
- Asparagus, carrots, fennel, onions, turnips, and sunflowers can stop potatoes from forming tubers.

• Never plant potatoes in the ground where anything else in the nightshade family, such as tomatoes or eggplant, was planted the year before.

There are lots of helpful plants for potatoes, though:

• Beans, corn, and cabbage planted around the potato hills help improve tuber growth and taste.

• Spinach and lettuce can be planted between rows to save room and because they won't strip the ground of nutrients.

• Basil, chamomile, thyme, parsley, and yarrow improve potato growth and taste and attract beneficial insects, as do alyssum and petunias.

Some plants will attract beneficial insects while others keep the pests at bay:

• Lamium not only improves growth and flavor but also deters bad insects.

• Sage will keep flea beetles at bay.

• Coriander, nasturtium, catmint, and tansy keep potato beetles away.

- Green beans keep potato bugs away and put nitrogen into the soil; in return, the potato plant keeps the Mexican beetle away from the beans.

- Marigolds deter many harmful insects and also keep bacterial and viral pests away.

Chapter 10: Potato Pests and Diseases – How to Handle and Prevent Them

No plant is immune to diseases or pests, and the potato is no exception. This chapter will help you identify what may be attacking your plants and tell you how to deal with it. It is worth noting that, while many people think that diseases and pests only manifest in large farms, where acres of potato plants grow together, the home gardener can also experience them too.

Bacterial Diseases

Bacterial Ring Rot – *Clavibacter michiganensis*

Symptoms

- Stems and leaves are wilting
- Leaves are dying
- The lower leaves begin to wilt first
- When you cut the tuber crossways, you see a ring of rot, creamy yellow to brown in color.

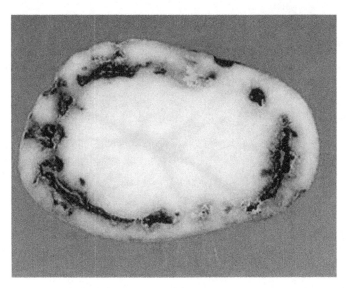

Cause

This is caused by a tuber-borne bacterium. This bacteria can get into the potato via cut wounds on the tuber, especially where your soil is warm and wet. The bacterium can also survive the winter in potato debris.

Management

When you purchase your seed potatoes, ensure they are certified as disease and virus-free. These are grown in beds where there is no ring rot. When you harvest your potatoes, make sure all potato debris is removed from the soil and ensure the equipment and tools you use are sanitized regularly.

Blackleg – also called soft rot – *Erwinia carotovora*

Symptoms

- The base of the stem that comes from the seed potato has small lesions on it, soaked in water.
- The lesions may get bigger, forming an extended lesion that runs from the stem base to the plant canopy.
- The plant tissue is water-soaked, soft, and anywhere between light brown and a dark, inky black.

- The leaves curl and wilt, and when they get wet, they are soft and slimy to the touch.

Cause

This is caused by bacteria on the tubers and in wounds on the plant. When you handle infected tubers to plant or cut them ready for planting, the bacteria can be spread to healthy tubers. This bacteria prefers very warm soil temperatures.

Management

The seed pieces you plant should be produced from tissue culture. Your tools and equipment should be sanitized regularly, especially when cutting potatoes for planting. Try not to damage the potatoes when you harvest them and ensure the leaves don't stay wet permanently by leaving enough time for the leaves to dry out thoroughly after watering.

Common Scab – *Streptomyces spp.*

Symptoms

- Raised lesions on tubers, brown and corky in texture
- Deep pitted lesions on the tuber, black or brown with a translucent, straw-colored tissue underneath

Cause

This is caused by a bacterium and is prevalent during warmer and dryer conditions.

Management

Managing and preventing common scabs is difficult because it takes a combination of several methods, which include:

- Making sure your seed tubers are not infected.
- Using crop rotation – not planting potatoes in the same place for three to four years between plantings.
- While no variety is immune to scab, you can purchase less susceptible varieties.
- Ensuring the soil has a high moisture content for between four and six weeks after the stolon tips begin swelling at the start of the tuber development.
- Amending soil, so it has a lower pH.
- Using the right fungicides to treat the potatoes at the right time.

Fungal Diseases

Black Dot - *Colletotrichum coccodes*

Symptoms

- Tiny black dots on the stems, stolons, and tubers – these are the fungal fruiting bodies
- Roots rotting beneath the ground
- Leaves turning yellow and wilting
- Defoliation

Cause

This is caused by a fungal disease that favors high temperatures and soil that drains poorly and is not properly aerated. The symptoms will be more severe where the soil is coarse and has little nitrogen in it.

Management

Ensure your plants are not stressed as they are more susceptible to the disease. Don't plant tubers or seed potatoes already infested, and make sure you water and fertilize the plants regularly. You can apply protective fungicides as well.

Black Scurf and Rhizoctonia Canker – *Rhizoctonia solani*

Symptoms

- Dark brown or black fruiting bodies on the potato surface, flat and irregularly shaped
- Sprouts may have sunken lesions, red-brown to black
- The stems may be girdled by the lesion, making the leaves curl up and turn yellow

Cause

This is caused by a fungus that can be easily spread through infected soil or when infected tubers are planted. The disease is more likely to emerge in moist, cool soil.

Management

Like the common scab, there are no potato varieties that are completely resistant. Controlling it relies on reducing how much inoculum is in the tubers and the soil. You can do this by applying fungicide to the soil and the seeds. Also, do not plant seed potatoes too deep in colder soils and ensure you practice crop rotation.

Gray Mold – *Botrytis cinerea*

Symptoms

- Potato flowers have fuzzy, gray mold on them
- The leaves may have wedge-shaped lesions, tan-colored
- The stems may have a slimy brown rot on them, coming from the petiole
- Tubers infected with the disease are wrinkly with wet, soft tissue
- The tubers may also develop a fuzzy, gray growth

Cause

The cause is a fungus that tends to emerge more in cool temperatures with excessive humidity and shaded areas.

Management

The best way to manage this disease is to ensure you water and fertilize the plants adequately. You can also apply protective fungicides to prevent the disease, but this will not treat an already established infection.

Pink Rot - *Phytophthora erythroseptica*

Symptoms

- Plant growth may be stunted
- The leaves may wilt and /or die
- The tuber is markedly decayed
- The tubers may have dark brown eyes
- Cut tubers become pink after being exposed to the air between 20 and 30 minutes, before turning brown and then black

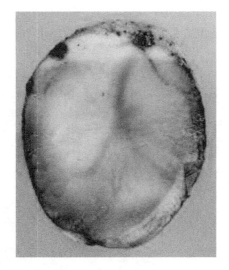

Cause

This disease is caused by a water mold known as an Oomycete. It emerges easier in soil heavily saturated with water later in the growing season.

Management

Potatoes should be planted in well-draining soil without a history of producing pink rot on potatoes. Do not overwater your plants, and try to avoid wounding the tubers during harvesting.

Potato Early Blight – *Alternaria solani*

Symptoms

- The leaves and stems may exhibit dark lesions that have yellow borders, like concentric rings of sunken and raised tissue.
- The lesions may start out circular but will become angular
- The leaves will stay attached to the plant but may be necrotic
- The tubers may have dry, dark lesions with a corky or leathery texture, and the margins will be a watery yellow-green color

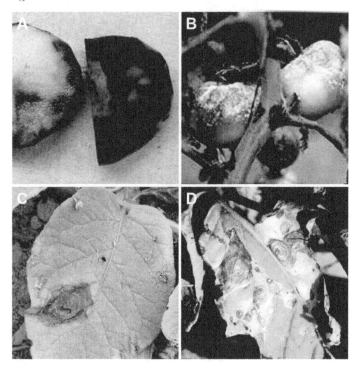

Cause

Caused by a fungus, the disease emerges when there is a cycle of dry and wet conditions where the leaves stay wet, and humidity is high.

Management

The easiest way to reduce the symptoms on the foliage is to apply the right protective fungicide. Fertilize and water the plants adequately to reduce the stress on them and try to plant late varieties that are not so susceptible to blight. Tubers should be stored in a cool, dry environment.

Powdery Scab – *Spongospora subterranea*

Symptoms

- Galls on the stolon and roots, white to brown in color
- Tubers have raised pustules on them, surrounded by the tuber skin
- The tuber may have shallow depressions with brown spores

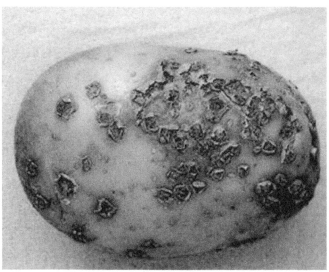

Cause

Caused by a fungal disease, where all the symptoms described above appear on the tubers, below the ground. The plant foliage is not affected.

Management

Avoid planting tubers that show signs of the disease. Make sure you plant your seeds in well-draining soil and, if the disease does occur, leave between three and ten years between planting potatoes in the same soil again. Do not plant tomatoes nearby.

Verticillium Wilt – *Verticillium dahlia, Verticillium albo-atrum*

Symptoms

- Plants will die early
- The leaflets will only die on one side of the branching stem or petiole
- When you cut the stem, you can see the tissue is discolored
- The tubers are discolored at the stem end

Cause

This is caused by a fungus that prefers to emerge early in the season during high temperatures and high moisture levels in the soil. Uninfected plants can become infected when infected soil moves or the wind moves infected plants against them.

Management

The best way to manage this is to plant potato varieties resistant to the disease. You can also practice furrow irrigation and make sure not to over-water your plants.

Viral Diseases

Potato Leaf Roll (PLRV)

Symptoms

- Young leaves are rolled up and turn pink or yellow
- The lower leaves roll upward and turn leathery
- The tuber may present with necrotic netting in the tissue
- The plant grows straight up instead of spreading and may be stunted in growth

Cause

Caused by a viral disease that numerous aphid species can transmit, infected seeds and plants may also feed the virus with inoculum.

Management

Ensure you purchase seed potatoes or plants cloned from PLRV-free stocks. In temperate regions, the harvest should be brought in early to avoid late-season migrations of aphids. Any tubers and plants infected must be removed and destroyed, and insecticides may be applied to help stop the disease from spreading.

Potato Virus A (PVA)

Symptoms

- The leaves may exhibit a mottling or mosaic pattern
- Plants with a severe infection may show patterns of alternating dark green and yellow tissue
- The leaves may look shiny
- The stems may bend slightly outwards

Cause

A viral disease transmitted by multiple aphid species. It may also be transmitted onto the next generation of tubers if infected tubers are planted. The disease shows only in the leaves, not in the tubers.

Management

Try to plant seed potatoes certified as free of PVA and choose PVA-tolerant varieties in regions where the disease is widespread. Systemic insecticide applications can help to control aphids.

Potato Virus X (PVX)

Symptoms

- The leaves show mild mosaic patterning
- Plants with a severe infection may have much smaller leaves
- The plant tops and the tubers may show necrosis

Cause

A viral disease. PVX is transmitted via infected leaves when they come into contact with healthy ones.

Management

The only to control PVX is to plant seed potatoes certified free of the disease.

Potato Virus Y (PVY)

Symptoms

This disease has a wide variety of symptoms, and your plants may have one or more of these:

- Mild mosaic patterning on the leaves
- Necrosis of the leaf and the plant dying – depends on the potato variety and disease strain
- You may see the symptoms on one shoot or more
- Where the leaves have severe necrosis, the tuber skin may have brown rings on it

Cause

A viral disease that can be transmitted by over 25 different species of aphids. The aphids can carry the disease over long distances, so the disease can spread far and wide. The disease can also be transmitted when infected plants or tubers come into contact with healthy ones.

Management

Make sure your seed potatoes are certified as PVY-free. Use systemic insecticides to help control the disease in your crop; however, it will not stop the infection from aphids. Any plants that show symptoms should be removed and destroyed to stop the spread. Where possible, plant PVY-resistant varieties.

Other Diseases

Leak - *Pythium spp*

Symptoms

- •Water-soaked area, tan-colored, around the wound on the tuber
- •The tuber rots internally, with the tissue turning spongy, with cavities forming in some cases
- •When the tuber is squeezed, it leaks a watery, dark liquid

Cause

This is caused by a fungal disease that can only get into the potato via cuts and wounds. Every cultivar is susceptible to it, especially in higher temperatures.

Management

The best way to manage this disease is to ensure crops are rotated and any infected tubers should be immediately destroyed. You can reduce the infection by applying foliar fungicides, and you can also leave the harvest until later, giving the tuber skin time to mature – this reduces the potential for injuries to the tubers.

Potato Late Blight – *Phytophthora infestans*

Symptoms

- The leaves show oddly shaped lesions, brown-colored, with fluffy white sporulation at the margins of the legions on the leaf's underside in wetter conditions.
- In drier conditions, the lesions will dry out, turning dark brown and showing collapsed tissue
- The stems may have water-soaked lesions, dark brown to dark green, also with the white sporulation
- In late-stage infections, the petioles and leaves will rot completely
- Plants with a severe infection may smell slightly sweet
- The tubers will show red-brown lesions going a few centimeters into the flesh
- The lesions may look sunken and will often result in bacterial rotting

Cause

This is caused by an Oomycete disease and can survive from a few months to several years in the soil. The disease emerges when conditions are cool and moist, and one of the biggest disease spreaders are infected tubers.

Management

Controlling late blight depends on several methods simultaneously, although some practices will differ depending on location. All volunteer plants should be destroyed, and the right fungicide should be applied to the potato hills when the plants emerge. Water early in the day, giving the leaves a chance to dry out throughout the day and try to plant blight-resistant varieties. If your region forecasts blight, use a protective fungicide.

Potato Pests

Diseases aren't the only thing to attack your potatoes; you also need to be on the lookout for these pests. Not all regions will experience many of these pests, but be aware of them, just in case.

Aphids – Peach Aphid (*Myzus persicae) and* Potato Aphid (*Macrosiphon euphorbiae*

Symptoms

• Tiny insects with soft bodies on the plant stem and /or the underside of the leaves

  • The insects are typically yellow or green, but some species may be brown, pink, black, or red – this also depends on the host plant

  • Where aphid infestations are heavy, the leaves may become distorted and /or turn yellow with necrotic spots, and the shoots may be stunted

  • You may see a sugary, sticky substance on the leaves or stem – this is honeydew and is secreted by the aphids and can lead to sooty mold growing on your plants.

Uncontrolled, aphids can lead to huge amounts of damage to potatoes because they transmit viruses like potato leaf roll (PLRV). Distinguishing features of the aphids are tubular structures known as cornicles projecting backward from the aphid's body, and when disturbed, the aphid rarely moves quickly.

Management

Where the aphid infestation is on only a few shoots or leaves, you can prune these out to prevent them from spreading. Before you plant any transplants, check for aphids before doing so. Where possible, plant resistant varieties and use reflective mulch, such as silver plastic – this deters the aphids from dining on your plants. If your plants are sturdy, use a strong water jet to push the aphids off the plant. You only need to use insecticides when the infestation is widespread because the plants will usually put up with low to medium infestation levels with no real adverse effects. One of the best methods of control is to use an oil like canola, neem oil, or an insecticidal soap – do follow the package guidelines exactly as written.

Colorado Potato Beetle – *Leptinotarsa decemlineata*

Symptoms

• You will see holes in the leaves where the beetles have been feeding

• Left untreated or in cases of severe infestation, the entire plant can be decimated

• The adult Colorado beetle is striped with yellow and black

• The larvae are red and have black heads at hatching, shortly changing to pink with black spots in two rows.

Adult beetles emerge in the spring when the female Colorado beetle will lay her eggs in batches of two dozen or less. They are orange-yellow, and you will see them on the undersides of the potato leaves. One female can lay over 500 eggs over four to five weeks.

Management

This is one of the most challenging and most damaging of all potato pests because, over time, they have developed a high level of resistance against insecticides. Planting the early maturing potato varieties can help you escape the most damage. When you see the beetles on your plants, you must hand-pick them off and drop them into a container of soapy water to kill them – dropping them in ordinary water will not help. You can also use heavy straw mulch around the base of your plants or use floating covers – the first makes it more difficult for the beetles to emerge from the ground, while the second makes it difficult for the beetle to fly to your plants. Some insecticides, such as Spinosad, may still be effective, but the best way is to monitor the plants daily and pick off the beetles and larvae as you see them. When you see eggs on the leaves, remove the entire leaf and drop it in soapy water.

Cutworm – *Agrotis spp* – *may include Peridroma saucia and Nephelodes minians.*

Symptoms

> • Young seedlings and transplants may have their stems severed at the soil surface

> • Later infections show as large holes in the surface of the tuber

> • Cutworm larvae are more active at night, hiding during the heat of the day in the soil around the plant base or, where plants have been toppled, they may also hide in the debris.

> • The larvae are approximately one to two inches in length and may come in many colors and patterns. However, regardless of this, all cutworms will curl in the shape of a C when disturbed.

Cutworms don't just limit themselves to potatoes, sadly. They will also attack cruciferous vegetables, such as cabbages, and peppers, beans, tomatoes, carrots, celery, and so on.

Management

When you harvest your potatoes, ensure that all plant debris and residue are removed from the ground. If you don't do it then, do it at least two to three weeks before you plant your potatoes in the soil. This is very important if the previous crop grown in that area was another one that can host the cutworm, such as leguminous cover crops, beans, or alfalfa. When your potatoes begin to show above the ground, you can fit foil or plastic collars that cover three inches of the plant on and above the soil line and going a couple of inches down into the soil – this can stop the larvae from severing your plants. Larvae should be hand-picked off the plants after dark as that is when they are active. You can put a layer of diatomaceous earth around the plants, creating a barrier that cuts the cutworms as they crawl across it. You can also use insecticides if you are not growing your potatoes organically.

Flea Beetles – *Epitrix spp*

Symptoms

- Leaves have small pits or holes in them
- Younger plants and seedlings are more susceptible, and growth may be stunted
- If the damage is severe enough, it can kill the plant
- Flea beetles are tiny, no more than three mm and are dark-colored and often shiny
- When disturbed, the flea beetle will jump

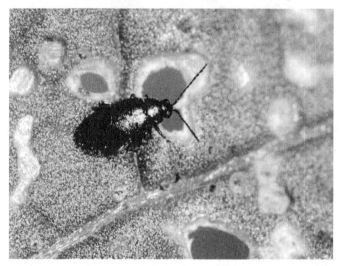

Flea beetles usually attack younger plants as the older, more established ones can tolerate the infestation. The beetles tend to overwinter on weeds. They stay in the soil and in plant debris and may go through three generations in one year.

Management

Where flea beetles are an issue, you may need to use floating row covers over your potato rows before the beetles emerge. This keeps the young plants protected from attack. You can also plant the seed potatoes early, allowing them to get more established before the beetles become too much of a problem – mature plants don't seem to have too many problems with the fleas and get little damage. You can also plant trap crops – cruciferous plants are the best ones as they attract the flea beetle - and keep them away from the potatoes. Layer mulch thickly around the potato plants to stop the beetles from getting to the soil's surface, and you can also use diatomaceous earth around the plants or spray with a neem oil solution. Insecticides can be used, including bifenthrin, carbaryl, permethrin, and Spinosad, but these are only effective for a week and must be reapplied – not suited to organic gardeners.

Wireworms – *Aeolus spp, Anchastus spp, Melanotus spp, Limonius spp*

Symptoms

- Seedlings may die
- Those that survive the initial attack will not stand straight, their stems are girdled, and they will show white
- The larvae hide in the soil around the stem and are yellow-brown, with shiny skin and are thin

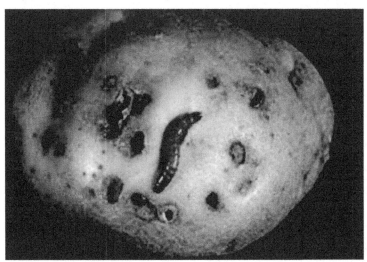

The wireworm can remain in a larval stage for up to five years, depending on which species it is, which makes it very hard to control.

Management

Standing crops cannot be chemically controlled; treatment needs to be applied before planting or used to treat the seed potatoes. If you know that wireworms are present in your soil in a fallow area where you plan to plant your potatoes frequently, till the soil to reduce their numbers. Where possible, rotate your crops to non-host plants and, where you have had a previous wireworm infestation, do not plant potatoes until the right treatment has been applied.

Note

You may have noticed that I recommended floating row covers as a form of treatment for some of these diseases and pests. For those that don't know, here's how to do that.

After planting your seed potatoes, watch for the first leaves to come through and then cover the row with a length of garden fleece or see-through plastic. It must be wide enough to allow the plants to grow beneath it. Use ground staples to hold the cover down, available online or from any garden center.

In terms of watering, if you can, lay a soaker hose beside the plants before you cover them – that way, you don't have to keep removing the cover to water and feed them.

When it comes time to hill up the potatoes, remove the staples on one side, hill up and replace the cover. When the plants start flowering, they will probably be at the stage where the cover is no longer adequate - it can now be removed, and your plants should be safe from most pests and diseases.

Pesticides

For so long, potatoes have been one of the staple crops in many gardens that provided an excellent source of carbohydrates in a vegetable you can do so much with. However, as we have mentioned, pests and diseases provide an ongoing battle for potato growers as they compete to destroy your crop before you can harvest it.

In this section, I want to discuss some of the chemical solutions available. However, because many gardeners prefer to grow organically, later, I will be giving you recipes for homemade solutions safe to use on your crops.

If you do choose to use these chemicals, please follow the instructions on the packs carefully.

Imidacloprid

Any pesticide that contains the active ingredient *imidacloprid* is suitable for use in any home garden. This chemical is designed to work on the potato and peach aphids that feed on the plant leaves and stems and spread the potato leafroll virus, amongst other diseases, that stunt the plant growth and reduce the harvest. It can also help fight the flea beetle larvae that feed on the tubers and roots. Imidacloprid is sprayed when the potatoes are planted to control insects in the soil.

• Warnings

However, imidacloprid may also contribute to spider mites and other pest outbreaks and is rated as moderately toxic to humans and animals. In terms of its toxicity rating for insects, it is moderately toxic to beneficial ones, and it will harm honeybees. It has a low toxicity rating for groundwater from the runoff.

Carbaryl

Carbaryl also works on the flea beetle larvae and some species of cutworm.

• Warnings

Carbaryl also goes by the name of Sevin and is rated as toxic (moderately) to humans and animals. It also has a moderate toxicity rating to groundwater from the runoff and is also moderately toxic to beneficial parasites and predatory mites. It has high toxicity to some beneficial predatory insects and will harm honeybees.

Dinotefuran

Less harmful to aquatic wildlife than the Imidacloprid or Carbaryl, dinotefuran insecticides help treat infestations of flea beetle larvae and whitefly, which both cause serious problems for crops in some parts of the USA.

• Warning

It has a very low toxicity rating for humans and animals and doesn't have such a hard impact on beneficial insects and bees.

Abamectin

Abamectin is a growing season insecticide that helps control many potato pests.

• Warning

It has a high toxicity rating for humans, animals, fish, and aquatic life and will also kill off beneficial insects like parasites, predatory mites, and bees.

Spinosad

Not as toxic as Abamectin, Spinosad is also designed to kill any pests that attack during the growing season. They target the pests as larvae when they are at their most vulnerable, protecting both the foliage and the tubers.

- **Warning**

Spinosad products are not so toxic to humans, animals, and other beneficial insects, and groundwater toxicity from runoff is also low. However, it is only toxic to insects and bees while the leaves remain wet, so it's best to spray at sun-down when the good insects have all gone for the day.

Cyfluthrin

Cyfluthrin products are designed to treat infestations of potato tuberworms that can destroy entire crops.

- **Warnings**

It has a low toxicity rating for humans and animals but a high rating for aquatic life and fish because of runoff. It is also highly toxic to honeybees and other beneficial insects.

Horticultural Oils and Soaps

Spider mite, aphid, and whitefly infestations can be treated using sprays made from horticultural oils or soap, which will smother the insect and kill it. These sprays will only target and kill the insect to the plant when sprayed and are far less toxic than the chemicals discussed above. Do make sure that you read the labels properly to ensure they can be used for food crops.

Herbicides

One of the main reasons herbicides are used is to remove weeds, which is a critical part of growing potatoes successfully. Weeds compete with your plants for water, nutrients, and light and can also be home to diseases and pests that affect your crops. By ensuring that you use preventive, cultural, and biological methods, you can remove the weeds from around your plants.

Biological control is all about using what Mother Nature provides. Many predators, such as millipedes, slugs, carabid beetles, field mice, crickets, and sowbugs, will devour weed seeds that lie on the soil's surface. By ensuring the seeds stay on the surface for longer, you give these predators a chance to eat more of them, thus reducing the seeds in the soil for a long time. Plus, if seeds are left on the surface, the winter months can bring about their decay.

Another good way of deterring weeds around your plants is hilling. As you hill up your potatoes, remove any growing weeds. The increased depth of soil around the plants will also prevent, or at least slow down, the growth of new ones. And using thick mulch layers around your plants will do the same thing.

However, using herbicides and other chemical controls is becoming more prevalent, but if you choose to use them, they should be used in conjunction with chemical-free methods.

Develop Your Program

This requires you to consider the weed species, what your soil is like, how you till and irrigate your ground, and the crop rotation methods you use. Most potato herbicides are limited in which weeds they can control.

Some herbicides must be applied to the soil, requiring manual watering or rainfall to move the herbicide into the soil to control the weeds. These are more often applied after the first hilling. Hilling will control some weeds that may appear if you don't use the soil herbicide.

If you applied the herbicide at the same time as you plant, you would need to reapply it later. By leaving the application until the first hilling, you get a much longer period of weed control. There are also herbicides you can apply to weeds that have already emerged.

However, herbicides are not recommended for use with garden farms as they are targeted towards large fields, covering one or more acres of potato plants. The best methods for home gardens are tilling, hilling, and hand weeding.

Organic Pesticides and Herbicides

Gardeners and farmers have traditionally sprayed their gardens and crops with chemicals to help control weeds, diseases, and pests. However, as time passes, we are all being made more aware of the dangers these chemicals pose to the wildlife in our gardens, and more people are choosing the organic route.

While pests and weeds are not pleasant to deal with, it's something that needs to be done. However, you can do it in a non-chemical way.

The rest of this chapter is devoted to homemade pesticides and herbicides you can use safely knowing that they will not harm you, your family, or pets, nor will they harm the beneficial insects that visit your garden.

Vegetable-Based Insecticide

Ingredients:

- ½ a cup of hot peppers
- ½ a cup of garlic cloves
- 1 large onion – white or yellow work best
- 2 cups of warm water

Instructions:

1. Place the peppers, onion, and garlic in your blender and blend them.
2. Pour into a bowl or jug.

3. Add the water, stir it and then leave it to stand for about 24 hours in a warm place.

4. Strain it into a spray bottle.

Use as needed as a pesticide on your potato plants.

Salt and Vinegar Herbicide

Ingredients:

- A gallon of vinegar
- A cup of salt
- A tablespoon of dish soap

Instructions:

1. Pour the salt into the vinegar and stir it thoroughly, ensuring all the salt has dissolved.

2. Add the dish soap and stir to incorporate.

3. Decant the mixture into spray bottles.

This will help with weed growth in the garden and on your patio. Apply only on cloudy days with no wind.

Orange Peel Pesticide

Ingredients:

- Peel from a whole orange
- 2 cups of boiling water

Instructions:

1. Put the peel in a bowl and pour the hot water over the top.

2. Leave it for at least 24 hours before removing the peel.

3. Strain the liquid into a spray bottle.

This helps eliminate insects on your plants.

Neem Oil Pesticide

Neem oil is commonly used as a natural insecticide, but it is harmful to pollinating insects. That doesn't mean it cannot be used, though; simply spray your plants in the evenings when the pollinators have gone and won't come back until the next day. The mixture is only harmful to them while the leaves are wet – once they dry off, the harm is neutralized.

As neem oil is sold in concentrated form, it should be diluted to a 1% or 2% concentration. Spray the leaves thoroughly, top and underside, and the stems. While it will not kill off any adult insects, it will kill the larvae. The spray will need to be reapplied throughout the season, but after a few sprayings, the insect lifecycle should have been disrupted. This is an excellent choice for the Colorado beetle and aphids.

Soap Insecticide

One of the simplest methods to kill insects on your plants is soapy water. It should be dish soap, not a perfumed soap with moisturizers in it, a simple mix at a ratio of three to five tablespoons per gallon of water. Sprayed on the plants, this will kill off most soft-bodied insects. However, if the Colorado beetle is attacking your plants, add a couple of drops of neem oil and spray at night after the pollinators have gone home.

Tips and Controls

Making the herbicide or pesticide is just one step in your aim to ensure your potatoes are pest and weed-free without a detrimental impact on the environment. These tips can get you all the way there:

> • Use a clean sprayer for each batch. If you use one that has previously had a different pesticide or herbicide in it, it

can be fatal to your crops. At the very least, you will get some dangerous and unpredictable results.

- Before you go spraying your newly made spray everywhere, test it on a small patch first. Spray a single plant or just a part of it and see what happens. This is most important when plants are stressed such as drought.

- Where you have small infestations of insects only, physical control works better. Pick the insects off the leaves and drown them in soapy water.

- If you have many aphids on your plants, use the hose pipe on a strong stream to knock them off. You can couple this with watering your potatoes, thus getting double the benefits.

- Learn to identify insects and distinguish between the good and the bad. If you see lots of beneficial predatory insects in your garden, there is a chance that your pest problem is under control or soon will be. Spraying indiscriminately may wipe out large numbers of these beneficial insects, and that will make your pest problem a whole lot worse.

- Try to introduce ladybugs and parasitic wasps to your garden when you see pests appear. Both feed on the bad bugs, and ladybugs are excellent for devouring Colorado beetle larvae.

- You can use floating row covers or netting over your plants to reduce the chances of the bugs actually making it onto your plants.

Chapter 11: Harvesting Your Potato Crops

You've made it this far. Your seed potatoes were successfully chitted, and where needed, cut and dried. You prepared your ground, dug your trenches or prepared your containers, and planted your potatoes. You hilled, watered, fertilized, and waited. You watched the sprouts grow into strong green stems, and now that they have died back, you know you were ready to harvest your bounty.

But what is the best way to harvest potatoes?

How to Harvest Your Spuds

There are a couple of ways to harvest potatoes. If you grew them in containers, you could just empty the container into a wheelbarrow or onto a tarpaulin and then root through the soil for the spuds.

With ground or raised bed growing, you can use shovels or spaces, pitchforks, and even hand tools, such as claws or trowels. Where your soil is nice and soft and not too deep, you can use your hands – do wear gloves, though.

Some of the larger garden tools, like spades, will cause some tubers to inevitably get chopped. Provided you only do this to a few, you can still use the potatoes, but they must be used right away.

If you are harvesting before your plants die off and the stems are still strong, you can pull the plant up – this won't work where your ground has gone too hard, though. Sometimes, you will find a few small potatoes still hanging onto the roots. To gather them, especially if you are waiting for the plant to die back completely, you must dig for them.

Dig gently a few inches away from the plant base and lift the soil. Make sure to get the potatoes that come with it. Sift through the soil to get every single potato and dig down, at least as deep as you've planted your seed potato, to make sure you don't leave any. If you leave them in the ground, they can rot, leave diseases, become a haven for pests or simply sprout again next year – right where you may not want spuds growing.

When to Harvest Your Spuds

The best time to harvest is based on the variety of potatoes grown, weather conditions, and whether you want new potatoes.

First Earlies

These are favored by most gardeners, as mentioned earlier, and include Lady Chrystl, Red Duke of York, Arran Pilot, and many more. These are the earliest type of potato to mature, and they are planted between St. Patrick's Day and mid-March, ready for harvest around 10 to 12 weeks later, usually June or July.

They are one of the easiest to grow, typically avoid being struck by blight, are tender and taste delicious, and are great to dig in the early summer days.

The first sign that the first early varieties are ready is when they flower. Most earlies will produce flower buds, but not all will bloom. When the unopened buds drop or the flowers begin to lose their color, you can start digging up your spuds. Mostly, these potatoes will be roughly egg-sized with tender skins.

If you are not sure if they are ready for harvest, dig gently around the plant to see if you can see the potatoes. If they are egg-sized or larger, you can harvest them. However, if you prefer to leave them, they will just continue growing. So, if you aren't sure if they are ready, just leave them a while longer. Mostly, early varieties are not suited to storage but do your homework because some varieties can be stored.

Second Earlies

Second earlies are varieties such as Maris Piper, Nicola, Kestrel, and Jazzy, and the only way they differ from the first earlies is in their maturity dates – about three weeks later.

You can plant these when you plant your first earlies, but it's best to wait until the first official day of spring, late March. That way, you get a new batch of spuds about five weeks after you harvest your first earlies – a never-ending supply of tender, tasty potatoes.

The same harvest indications apply here – look for the flowers. When they fade or unopened blooms drop, the potatoes are ready to harvest.

Maincrop Potatoes

When you buy those big baking spuds in the grocery stores, they are likely a main-crop variety. These are best for storing and include Pink Fir Apple, Cara, Purple Majesty, King Edward, or, in the USA, the Russet varieties.

Typically, maincrops are planted at the same time, or up to a month after, as the first earlies and need about 20 weeks to grow. They will swell over the summer months, growing large harvests of large potatoes.

Although you can harvest these as early varieties or take a few after flowering, they are best left to mature fully. If you want earlies, grow the early varieties as they are specifically bred to crop early and have the texture and flavor you want. Maincrops should be left longer as they will store much better.

Maincrops are usually harvested from August through September, and you will know when it's time because the foliage will turn yellow and shrivel up before dying. At this point, chop the foliage down so only about an inch is showing and then leave the plant for a further two weeks, allowing the tubers to harden off, preparing them for storage.

This die-back process is natural and different from diseased potatoes. If the leaves have black spots on them or only part of the plants die off, you know it isn't natural. And if your plants die before the 20 weeks, there is also likely to be something wrong.

If you want new potatoes from your maincrop, wait until around one-third of the plant has died back. The potatoes will be smaller, and the skin is delicate, so they can easily be damaged with garden tools if you are not careful.

This is also a good time to check on the crop and see what's happening in terms of size and texture.

When you harvest your potatoes, get everything out of the ground, even the tiny ones. A farmer sold these in half-pint containers recently, calling them "peanut potatoes," and they are delicious dropped whole into the frying pan, roasted, or grilled. Because they have a high ratio of skin to flesh, they cook up wonderfully crispy.

A word of advice – if you grow in containers, raised beds, and in the ground, be sure to space your plantings for the maximum length of crop time.

Hardening Your Potatoes Off

If you want firmer potato skins or intend to store them over the winter, you can leave them in the ground up to one month after the foliage has died. Do not water them, though; they must be kept dry otherwise, they can rot or resprout.

If the forecast hints at frost or heavy rain, harvest the potatoes immediately, even if they haven't finished hardening off under the ground. However, you can take them indoors to complete the hardening-off process.

Storing Your Potatoes

This chapter is followed by another on potato storage, so I won't go into much detail here. What I will say is, brush excess dirt off your potatoes and keep them in a cool, dry, dark place indoors.

They can be stored for up to two months in the refrigerator, so long as they are in a Ziploc bag or wrapped in plastic. You can store washed and unwashed potatoes this way, but if you choose to wash them, they must be dried before storage. Otherwise, they may rot.

Do not wash hardened potatoes for long-term storage. Leave them to dry outdoors if it's dry and cloudy or indoors if the weather is wet.

Any that have wounds from the tools used to harvest them can be used immediately – they will not store.

If you are storing different-sized potatoes, use the smaller ones first as they don't keep so long.

Potato Tips

These are just a couple of pro-tips:

Do NOT Eat Green Potatoes

If you notice that any of your spuds have green skin, do not eat them. They have been exposed to the light, and this will increase the alkaloid levels in the potato, creating solanine, a toxin that is poisonous to us and makes the potatoes taste bitter.

To avoid this, potatoes should be properly hilled up during the growing process and kept in a dark place once harvested.

Potatoes that only have a tiny hint of green can still be eaten, so long as the green is completely cut off.

Don't Eat Potato Seeds

As your plants mature, you may see what looks like unripe cherry tomatoes on them before they begin dying off. These are potato seeds and must not be eaten – they are poisonous.

You could save them and plant them the following year, but you won't get the same strain of potato. Potatoes never grow true from seeds, and propagation is done by keeping seed potatoes from a harvest to plant the following year. However, this is one way for diseases to be passed on through the plants, so the recommendation is to purchase new seed potatoes every year.

Rotate Your Crops

When you grow potatoes and tomatoes in the garden, ensure that you have them on a three-year rotation plan. That means you need three separate areas, with one being left fallow every year. That way, the soil won't get too exhausted, and there is less chance of pests and diseases hiding in the soil. Neither crop should ever be planted in the same place two years running.

Chapter 12: How to Store Your Potatoes

You've finished the hard work of growing, maintaining, and harvesting your potatoes, and you dream of creamy mash, crispy home fries, and delectable baked potatoes. But let's be honest here, there really is only so much potato you can eat. If you don't want your hard work to go to waste, you need to think about how you will store your potatoes to keep you going through the winter, right through to when you can begin harvesting again next year.

Luckily, people have been doing this for years, and you can now reap all the rewards of their hard work and experiments. There are several ways to store your potatoes, and here are five of the best ways.

Storage in a Root Cellar

This is the traditional way of storing potatoes, placing them somewhere cool, dark, and dry where they cannot freeze – the root cellar.

If you are not lucky enough to have a root cellar, you can just as easily use a corner of an unheated garage or your basement. However, just throwing them in there and hoping for the best won't work. First, they must be prepped, and that requires a curing process that can take several days.

Sorting and Curing Your Potatoes

Once your harvest is in, you need to sort through all your potatoes and put aside those best suited to be stored. Straight out of the ground, potatoes don't have tough enough skin to protect them from rot, so you must take the utmost care when you handle them, ensuring you do not cut or bruise them in any way.

The best potatoes for storage are large ones with no blemishes or puncture marks – tiny wounds may heal during the curing process, but large ones won't. If you have potatoes with moderate to excessive damage, they should be consumed within a couple of days, used for another purpose, or stored using a different method.

It's also worth remembering that not all varieties are equal when it comes to storage. The best ones are brown potatoes and russets with thick skins, rather than the red-skinned and fingerling varieties.

Preparing your potatoes for storage is easy enough – simply rub off the excess dirt and lay them on newspaper. They must not touch each other and should be left somewhere dark and cool for about two weeks. This will harden off the skins, allowing the potatoes to last for a longer time once in storage. Do NOT wash them beforehand – they store better left unwashed, dry, and a bit dirty.

Storing Cured Potatoes

Once your potatoes are cured, they can be stored in any container with ventilation – cardboard boxes, laundry baskets, crates, paper bags, hessian sacks, etc.

Do NOT use plastic as it promotes the retention of moisture and your potatoes are likely to rot.

When it comes to storing, you can now allow your potatoes to touch, although many people do use shredded paper or another buffer material. This helps insulate the potatoes and stops rot and disease from spreading should one potato "fall ill."

The potatoes can be stores in a root cellar or similar dark and cool room, at a temperature of 35 to 40°F. Do not put them in the refrigerator – refrigerated air is dry and will cause your potatoes to shrivel. The only time you should store potatoes in the refrigerator is when you intend to use them within a few days.

Cover your storage containers with cardboard, fleece, or another material and, if necessary, cut a few ventilation holes in them.

Check on your potatoes every couple of weeks and remove any that have started sprouting or are starting to go soft. If you don't do this, you might be shocked at how quickly one rotten potato can destroy the entire contents of the container. And if you have ever smelled a rotten potato, you'll know it's a smell you will never forget.

Troubleshooting

Potatoes can last for up to eight months if they are stored properly. But things can go wrong, especially with those new to this, so, for the best chances of success, follow these guidelines:

- Do NOT store potatoes near fresh fruit, especially apples. Fruit gives off ethylene gas, and this can cause your potatoes to start sprouting or rotting.

- Stored potatoes often taste a little sweeter because their starch is slowly being converted to sugars. Stop this from having an impact on your meals by removing the potatoes from storage a few days before you want to cook them. This will cause the sugars to turn back to starch.

- If your potatoes are exposed to any light, they will develop green skin, which is bitter and toxic. Cut off the green before cooking.

- Unless you intend to keep some potatoes as seed potatoes, remove any sprouts you see on your stored potatoes.

Reburying Your Potatoes Outdoors

If your storage goals are not quite so ambitious and all you want is for your potatoes to last a couple of months, there is a very simple method to get you through the late fall. Simply place your potatoes straight back in the ground when you have harvested them.

To do this, dig broad trenches, around six inches deep, and lay your potatoes at the bottom. Cover them with a little loose soil and some straw or a thick wad of newspaper to give them protection against rainfall.

This way, you can keep your potatoes fresh until you are ready to dig them up again in the fall.

You might wonder why you can't just leave them in the ground and not harvest them at all. The simple answer is, if they are left attached to a dead plant, they will rot.

And, if you opt to place your potatoes in a root cellar after digging them up again, you could potentially extend their lifespan by several months.

Slicing, Blanching, and Freezing

If you have space in your freezer, you can store some of your potatoes in there. It is a more convenient method than canning, and you can store potatoes this way for up to a year, beating root cellars hands down.

First, peel your potatoes and submerge them completely in cold water – there must be no part left uncovered. Otherwise, it will turn brown. Larger potatoes should be chopped, so they are all approximately the same size – this ensures they cook evenly.

Bring a large pot of water up to a rolling boil. Rinse the potatoes and put them in boiling water. Leave them to blanch for between three and five minutes, depending on what size they are.

While they are blanching, prepare a large bowl of ice water. Remove the potatoes from the hot water using a slotted spoon and plunge them straight into the ice water. This will immediately stop the potatoes from cooking, and they will not turn mushy.

Once they are cool, drain them and put them in a good-quality freezer bag. If you have a vacuum sealer, even better as you need to remove as much air as possible from the bag.

You can also make your own home fries in this way. Simply cut the potatoes into chips and follow the same method.

When you want the potatoes, remove them from the freezer and defrost them. This works better if you leave them in the refrigerator overnight as you get a much better texture than if you use the microwave to defrost them.

Potatoes can be frozen in many ways. You can cube them, shred them, scallop, mash, bake, or even fry them.

Pressure Canning

Potatoes can also be canned to store for longer periods without relying on refrigeration. You will need a pressure canner for this – water bath canners cannot get to the high temperatures needed to store these safely.

You will also need some sterilized, quart-sized mason jars, your potatoes, and salt. Peel your potatoes, making sure to cut any eyes out. Chop the potatoes into chunks of about half-inch and submerge them in a bowl of cold water.

Bring a pot of water to a boil and blanch them for three to five minutes. Drain and rinse the potatoes to wash off any starch, and then place them in the mason jars. Fill the jars with hot water, making sure you leave an inch of space at the top. Add a teaspoon of salt to each jar for taste if you want to.

Wipe the rims, cap them with clean rings and lids, and then pressure the can for 40 minutes at a pressure of 10 pounds.

Dehydrating Potatoes for Potato Flakes

This option is perfect for those willing to put in the work, as your harvest can be preserved pretty much indefinitely if you dehydrate them into flakes.

Start by washing your potatoes and peeling them. Cook them until you can cut a knife easily through them – the mushier, the better.

Leave the water to cool and then mash the potatoes – don't drain them, mash them in the water. You can use an immersion blender in the pot or transfer them to a stand mixer to blend them into a silky smooth mixture.

Spoon the potatoes onto a dehydrator sheet – the thinner the sheets are, the quicker the potatoes will dry. Set your dehydrator to 140 degrees and check on them after about 12 hours.

When the potato breaks rather than bends, they are ready. You must be patient, though, as this can take upwards of 36 hours.

Once the potatoes are dry, place them in a food processor and pulverize them. They can then be stored in airtight containers.

To rehydrate the potatoes, you can add a tablespoon of butter and 2/3 of a cup of milk to a pan and bring it to a boil. Turn off the heat and add a further ¼ cup of milk and 2/3 of a cup of potato flakes. As they begin to rehydrate, add more milk and butter as you want.

There are a couple of other ways you can dehydrate your potatoes for storage – slicing or shredding.

First, wash your potatoes and remove any blemishes – whether you peel them is up to you. Slice them to about 2.5 mm thick using a sharp knife or a mandolin, keeping the thickness consistent. Alternatively, use the coarse side of your grater to shred the potatoes.

Immediately submerge your sliced or shredded potatoes in cold water to stop them from turning brown while you bring a large pot of water to the boil. Blanch the potato for a few minutes or until fork tender. If you do not do this, the potatoes will go grey-black when they are rehydrated – not poisonous but not nice to look at.

Use a slotted spoon to remove your potatoes or strain them and lay them on dehydrator trays. Sliced potatoes should not overlap one another – shredded potatoes should be in as thin a layer as possible. Dry sliced potatoes for about eight to ten hours at 125°F – shredded potatoes won't take quite so long.

When done, the potatoes should be translucent and crisp. Leave them to cool and then store in airtight containers where they won't get crushed. To rehydrate sliced potatoes, drop them straight into casseroles, scalloped potatoes, or gratin recipes. Shredded potatoes can be soaked in water for 15 minutes, drained, and fried – great for making your own hash browns.

Troubleshooting Stored Potatoes

Every person who has stored potatoes has lost some or all of their storage to Pythium leak, pink rot, Fusarium dry rot, or bacterial soft rot. These are the four most serious pathogens that can cause serious storage losses, and they may be brought in on tubers with the diseases, or they can survive on debris in storage. Most will destroy a tuber within a few weeks and then quickly spread throughout the rest of the pile.

Where conditions are dry, soft and pink rot are less prevalent, but other issues may be caused by dry conditions, high temperatures, and early maturity. Paying attention to your harvest, the curing process, and how you handle your potatoes can help maintain your storage quality.

Two major factors in helping to reduce losses like this are allowing the skins to mature under the ground before you harvest and keeping your storage area free of moisture. However, some tubers may already be infected with silver or black scurf and, the longer they stay in the soil, the more severe the infection is. To avoid these, harvest your potatoes as soon as the skins have set. If the weather is wet during the harvest season, the soil will likely stick to the tubers, promoting the right conditions for soft rot.

The optimum time for harvesting potatoes is when they are at pulp temperature, allowing for successful storage. These temperatures will vary, depending on the ventilation system in the storage area, potato varieties, timeliness, and cool air availability. Based on where you harvest your potatoes in the summer, when the temperature is 80°F or above, and they can cool down slowly, there is a much higher chance of rot setting in when the potatoes are stored.

Those potatoes destined for refrigerated storage can be harvested at a pulp temperature of between 62 and 65°F as a maximum. Non-refrigerated storage potatoes should not have a pulp temperature of over 60°F. When you put your potatoes into storage, they will require humidity, fresh air, and temperatures of around 55°F for the preconditioning stage. Environmental conditions are much harder to handle if pulp temperatures are too high.

Try to time your harvest for when there is at least three to six hours of cool air outside. Where your harvest comes in later, try to do it before the temperatures drop below 45°F; otherwise, your potatoes are more susceptible to bruising.

Follow the guidelines below for harvesting and storing your potatoes to help prevent disease spreading and ensure your stored potatoes remain fresh:

Killing the Vines

• Killing the vines will prevent the tubers from growing any bigger, will stabilize the flesh, and help set the skin

• This can be done using chemical or mechanical methods, or a combination of both

• If you use a chemical desiccant, you may need two or more applications

• When the vines are killed off, tubers are easier to dig up and harvest.

Disease Management

• Late blight and other foliar diseases can still threaten your harvest, even when the vines are dying off, or you have implemented a method to kill them off. Pathogens such as these spread to the potato tubers and can cause many problems with stored potatoes if the disease is not controlled before the harvest.

• Rather than applying a desiccant and fungicide at the same time, it is best to apply the desiccant first, followed by the fungicide a few days later. That way, you ensure that the remaining plant material is thoroughly covered.

Skin Set

• Most diseases that affect tubers can enter a potato only via a wound. By ensuring the skin sets properly, you can ensure less wounding when you harvest the potatoes, and the stored potatoes are less likely to become diseased.

• Before you harvest your potatoes, allow the skin to set in the ground for at least 10 to 14 days.

Preventing Wounds and Bruising

• Ensure that the equipment you use to harvest and transport your potatoes is in good working order and will cause no major damage to your tubers,

• Make sure the soil is moist but not soaking wet when you harvest your potatoes. The pulp temperatures should be 60 to 65°F to protect the potatoes from bruising and wounding.

Grading

• Once your potatoes are harvested, sort through them quickly, ensuring the diseased and wounded are removed quickly. The longer healthy and wounded/diseased are together, the more chance there is of disease spreading.

Curing and Healing Period

• This should be done straight after harvest and is critical to your potato storage success.

• Tubers should be stored at a relatively high humidity of 95% and temperatures between 50 and 60°F for 10 and 14 days after harvest. This gives any wounds the time to heal before you put them into colder storage. Any storage less than 95% humidity will stop the wounds from healing.

• Ensure that your stored potato piles have sufficient airflow over them and between the potatoes. This ensures a constant supply of oxygen and stops condensation from storing. However, the potatoes should not be over-dried during this period.

Storage

• Before you store your potatoes, ensure the storage area is thoroughly cleaned and inspected. Ensure you have adequate insulation, humidifiers, and fans in place, and a good ventilation system. If any of your systems are not in place or not working properly, it can have a detrimental effect on your storage and can cause diseases to spread quickly.

• Once the curing period is finished, allow your potatoes to cool off to the temperature you want gradually – table stock and seed potatoes should be 38 to 40°F, chipping should be 45 to 50°F, and French fries should be 50 to 55°F.

30 Uses for Potatoes

While potatoes are a staple food in many people's homes, they can also be used for other things besides cooking. And being healthy to eat, they also have other good properties that make them one of the most useful vegetables there is.

In the Garden

First off, let's look at some ways you can use potatoes in your garden. Not only are the plants good to help break up the soil, but they are good companions for other plants too. But there are other things you can do with them:

One - Use potato scraps to grow more potatoes

When you peel your spuds, don't throw away the peelings. If you don't intend to place them on your compost heap, you can use the peelings to grow more potatoes, provided there are potato eyes on them.

Two - Use them as rose and geranium fertilizer

Some gardeners swear that potatoes are powerful enough to fertilize geraniums and roses, and it can be done in several ways. You can add the peelings and waste to your compost heap and then use it on your plants, or you can mulch the plants using potato peelings. However, another way involved cutting a hole into a large potato and popping a rose or geranium stem into it.

Plant the potato in a pot of compost, and the potato will fertilize the flower, giving it a great head start.

Three - Use potatoes to stop your greenhouse glass fogging up

Not only is foggy glass irritating to you, but it can also stop light from getting to your plants inside a greenhouse. Slice a potato in half and wipe the cut edges over the glass – this will stop them from becoming foggy.

Four - Use them to stop ice on glass cold frames and windshields

Using the same trick as the greenhouse glass, you can also do the same on car windshields and glass on outdoor cold frames to stop them from icing up.

Five - Potatoes can remove rust from tools

The last way to use potatoes in the garden is to get rid of rust on your garden tools. Simply cut a potato and rub the pieces over the tools. Leave it for a couple of minutes and then wipe it off – hey presto, the rust comes off with it.

In the Kitchen

This would seem the most obvious place to use potatoes but, aside from cooking them in several ways, you can also use them in these ways too:

Six - Use them to thicken stews, sauces, and gravy

Not only can you add potatoes to your soups and stews to eat, but you can also use them to thicken them up too. The first way is to add chunks of potato or some mashed potato into the soup or stew, but the second way is a little different. This involves making potato starch, which allows you to thicken up your sauces, etc., without adding a potato flavor. Here's how to do it:

- Line a colander using two bits of cheesecloth and place it over a bowl.
- Grate a potato in the colander – use the smallest holes on the grater.
- Fold the cheesecloth over the potato and press down on it until the starchy liquid comes out into the bowl.
- Open up the cloth and add half a cup of water to the potatoes.
- Cover and squeeze and then repeat with a further half a cup of water.
- After the second time, leave the cheesecloth closed and weigh it down for a couple of hours - a couple of cans will do the trick – to allow more starch to drain out.
- Discard the potato and the cheesecloth and pour the water into another bowl – be careful; you do NOT want to disturb the starch that has settled at the bottom.
- Leave that starch to dry out and store in an airtight container until you need it.

Seven – Make potato flour

You can also make your own potato flour – not the same as the potato starch as it is made using whole potatoes. Potato flour cannot really be used as a complete flour replacement, but it can be added to grain flour to make them go that little bit further. It also helps to add some moisture and a little taste to baked goods. Here's how to make it:

- Wash two potatoes and peel them.
- Slice them thinly – a mandolin slicer is the best thing to use.
- Arrange the slices on a tray or flat plate – not overlapping for faster drying.
- Leave the tray in the sunlight and leave it for about 30 to 45 minutes.
- Turn the potato slices over and leave them to completely dry. On a warm sunny day, this should take about three or four hours.
- Once dry, the potato slices should look crisp and white – if they crush easily between your thumb and finger, they are done.
- Grind the slices into a fine powder, sieve it, and then store it in airtight containers until you need it.

Two good-sized potatoes will provide approximately four tablespoons of flour.

Eight – Potatoes can reduce excess salt

If you add a bit too much salt to a stew or a soup, you need only to pop a few chunks of potato in and leave them for about 15 minutes. By then, they will have absorbed most of the salt, leaving your dish tasting as it should.

Nine – Potatoes can remove sticky substances or stains from hands

If you are preparing vegetables that stain or using honey or another sticky substance, rub a potato between your hands to remove the stains and stickiness. This works well for berry or beet stains and can make sticky substances less sticky and easier to clean.

Ten – make biodegradable plastic

This is one of the best uses – making biodegradable, eco-friendly plastic! Lots of manufacturers now use potato starch in bio-manufacturing, meaning waste is no longer an issue. Unlike traditional plastic, this one can simply be tossed on your compost heap, and it will decompose. Here's how you can make your own:

- First, extract the starch from a potato using the instructions above. If you intend to use it straight away, you need not dry it.

- Add four tablespoons of cold water to a pan.

- Add one tablespoon of the starch and mix it with the water.

- Add one teaspoon of vinegar and one teaspoon of vegetable glycerin and stir it all together – more glycerin makes the plastic soft and flexible, while fewer makes it hard and brittle.

- If you want colored plastic, add about five drops of food coloring and stir.

- Heat the mixture on low heat and stir it constantly. When it begins thickening, turn up the heat to medium and stir.

- When the mixture begins to boil, leave it for about five minutes – it needs to be a sticky mixture, a bit gooey.

- Pour the mixture onto a silicone pad or a sheet of aluminum foil and leave it to dry in a sunny place – it should take about 24 hours but, if you want it quicker, use an oven on 150°F for one to two hours.

To use this to make plant pots, simply mold it before it dries.

For Cleaning

Potatoes can also be used for cleaning.

Eleven – For removing stains from clothing or carpets

As well as helping remove stains from your hands, you can also use them to remove stains from fabrics, such as curtains, clothes, and carpets. Grate a raw potato and rub it over the stain before rinsing with warm water.

Twelve – For cleaning your windows

Potatoes don't only stop your greenhouse windows from fogging up; they can also be used to clean your house windows. Cut a potato in half and rub the cut side over the winds. Wipe with a clean rag for crystal clear windows.

Thirteen – Use them to shine your silver

If silver items are tarnished or dirty, simply soak them in the water you used to boil potatoes. Leave them for around 30 minutes and then drain and rinse them, leaving them looking as shiny as new.

Fourteen – Potatoes make good shoe-shiners

If you rub a cut potato over leather shoes, it can leave them looking nice and clean. Simply wipe the potato off using a damp rag and then, if required, polish the shoes.

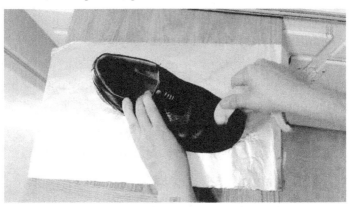

Fifteen – Absorb moisture with potato starch

In storage spaces that might get damp, leave a couple of bowls or breathable sachets of potato starch – they will absorb moisture, leaving the place smelling nice and free of damp.

For Beauty and Cleansing

It might surprise you to learn that potatoes can be used for your beauty and cleansing regime, and in natural DIY products.

Sixteen – Use potatoes to make soap

When you make soap using potatoes, it will leave your skin smooth and silky. Here's one way to do it:

Ingredients:

- A large potato
- A bar of soap – Dove works well for this
- 1 spoon of Aloe gel
- 1 spoon of almond oil

Instructions:

- Peel and grate the potato into a cheesecloth or muslin cloth.
- Squeeze the juice out.
- Grate the soap onto a bowl and add the potato juice.
- Add the almond oil and Aloe gel and mix it all together.
- Place a large pan of water on to heat.
- Place the soap ingredients into a heatproof bowl inside the pan and stir the contents over high heat.
- Pour the mixture into a glass and leave it for several hours to cool – it should easily slide out of the glass.
- Store it somewhere cool and dry and use it whenever you have a shower.

Adding potato to soap helps brighten your skin. The antioxidants in the potato juice help rejuvenate your cells, making your skin look brighter.

Seventeen – Use potato starch to make deodorant

Potato starch can be added to natural deodorant, helping to soak up moisture:

Ingredients:

- 2 tablespoons potato starch
- 2 tablespoons baking soda
- 3 tablespoons organic coconut oil, softened

Instructions:

- Mix the starch and baking powder together in a small bowl.
- Stir in the coconut oil, incorporating it into a creamy, smooth mixture.
- Transfer the mixture to a small food-grade container – silicone muffin liners are a great choice – and refrigerate until hard, a few hours.
- Pop the deodorant out of the containers and use it as you would any other roll-on deodorant stick.
- Store it in the refrigerator in an airtight container if you want the rub-on texture or, if you prefer a creamy lotion, store it at room temperature.

Eighteen – Use potato to remove bags or circles under your eyes

Slice a potato and lay a slice over each eye. It helps remove puffiness and bags or dark circles.

Nineteen – Make a cleanser and toner to get rid of acne

Potatoes are acidic, astringent, and drying, making them great for greasy skin and acne. Simple wipe potato juice over your face or target individual blemishes. Repeat daily for the best results.

Twenty – Make a potato facial mask

Blend potato with natural yogurt and spread it over your face. Leave it for 15 minutes and rinse off thoroughly, leaving you with a glowing complexion.

For Minor Ailments and Good Health

This works because potatoes are good for cleansing and beauty treatments. While some of these may be classed as "old wives tales" and check with your doctor where you are in any doubt, you can use potatoes for these:

Twenty-One – Helping to heal burns, bruises, and sprains

Some say that potato juice applied to sunburns or bruises can help the area to heal quicker and remove skin discoloration more quickly too. For sprains, some say that you can run potato juice over the sprain before you wrap it to help it heal.

Twenty-Two – Soothing itchy or sore skin

Where you have insect bites, sunburn, or other minor skin itches, rubbing potato juice in can help soothe them.

Twenty-Three – Relieving headaches

There are people who say you can relieve a headache by rubbing a raw potato across your temples.

Twenty-Four – To help you sleep

One folk remedy says that if you mix mashed potatoes with milk and consume it before you go to bed, it will help you sleep better.

Twenty-Five – To make cold or hot compresses

Boil a potato for a hot compress or freeze a cooked one for a cold compress. Wrap it in a cloth and apply it where and when needed.

Many of these are considered old wives tales, and there is no guarantee they will work.

Other Unusual Uses

Lastly, a few miscellaneous uses for potatoes:

Twenty-Six – To generate power

You might have tried this as a kid at school, but if not, you can draw a certain amount of power from a potato. The water in a potato is an electrolyte and can generate some electricity when used with copper and zinc electrodes. You can use them for powering light bulbs or other small devices. If you boil a potato for eight minutes, you will get ten times more power than if you use a raw one. It might interest you to know that you can light up one room in your house for more than a month with a potato battery!

Twenty-Seven – Safely remove a broken lightbulb

If a lightbulb breaks in its fitting, you can use a potato to remove it safely. First, ensure the light switch has been turned off, and then use pliers to remove any glass left on the bulb – don't forget eye protection! Cut a potato in half and press it against the socket firmly. Twist it counter-clockwise, and the potato should get a grip on the bulb base, pulling it out.

Twenty-Eight – Reduce Fogging on Glasses and Goggles

Even on diving masks – rub the cut side of a potato over the glass to stop it from fogging.

Twenty-Nine – Make Craft and Decorating Stamps

Potatoes are great for stamps. Carve the design you want in a raw potato, dip it in ink or paint and stamp away to your heart's content. This can be used for printing on fabric, furniture, clothes, walls, and so on.

Thirty – Make potato print clothes and curtain

Using the potato stamps, you can create your own unique designs in just about any fabric you want.

All of these uses for potatoes are designed for potatoes that would otherwise be discarded, such as blemished, cut, or green potatoes you wouldn't otherwise eat.

Conclusion

Thank you for taking the time to read my guide. I hope you found it helpful and that it will encourage you to start growing your own potatoes.

While growing potatoes may seem like a relatively easy task, as you have now discovered, there is much more to it to ensure a good healthy harvest and a stream of new potatoes in the spring and summer, with plenty to store over the winter months.

Like any plant, potatoes need a certain amount of care and maintenance to ensure the best success, and this book has attempted to show you exactly what you need to do. You are also not confined to the traditional method of growing potatoes in the ground. These days, more people are choosing containers and raised beds, partly because of a lack of space and partly because they are easier to care for. I use all three methods – I have my early potatoes growing in containers and potato bags, second earlies in raised beds, and my maincrops go into the ground. That way, I know I have potatoes on hand from June right through to the winter months.

How you grow yours is up to you, but you should experience great success if you follow the basic guidelines offered in this book. And, if you have never grown your own potatoes before, trust me when I say you won't ever purchase shop-bought spuds again. There's nothing like the taste of new potatoes fresh from your own plot in the summer and large bakers freshly dug from the ground in the fall.

All that remains is for me to wish you the very best of luck in your potato-growing endeavor!

Here's another book by Dion Rosser that you might like

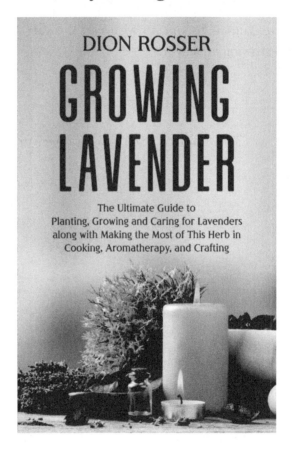

References

A New Strategy: Growing Potatoes in Straw - Properly Rooted. (n.d.). Retrieved from https://properlyrooted.com/growing-potatoes-straw/

admin. (2015, January 21). *Potato Harvest and Storage.* Center for Agriculture, Food and the Environment. https://ag.umass.edu/vegetable/fact-sheets/potato-harvest-storage

Albert, S. (2009, January 20). *How to Plant and Grow Potatoes.* Harvest to Table. https://harvesttotable.com/how_to_grow_potatoes/

August 10, & To, 2014 in H. (2014, August 10). *Natural Pesticides and Herbicides You Can Make.* Envirobond Products Corp. https://www.envirobond.com/how-to/natural-pesticides-herbicides-recipes-make

Growing Potatoes In Containers & Pots. (2021, January 22). Kellogg Garden Organics™. https://www.kellogggarden.com/blog/gardening/container-gardening/growing-potatoes-in-containers-and-pots/

Growing Potatoes the No-Dig Way. (n.d.). GrowVeg. Retrieved from https://www.growveg.co.uk/guides/growing-potatoes-the-no-dig-way/

How and when to harvest potatoes: know when to dig potatoes up. (2020, June 19). Lovely Greens. https://lovelygreens.com/when-to-harvest-potatoes

How and Why You Should Chit Your Potatoes. (2017, April 14). Julia Dimakos. https://www.juliadimakos.com/how-to-chit-your-potatoes/

How to Care For Potatoes - GardenFocused.co.uk. (n.d.). Www.gardenfocused.co.uk. Retrieved from https://www.gardenfocused.co.uk/vegetable/potatoes/potatoes-care.php

How to grow potatoes. (n.d.). BBC Gardeners' World Magazine. Retrieved from https://www.gardenersworld.com/how-to/grow-plants/how-to-grow-potatoes/

How To Grow Potatoes In Bags | Thompson & Morgan. (n.d.). Www.thompson-Morgan.com. Retrieved from https://www.thompson-morgan.com/how-to-grow-potatoes-in-bags#:~:text=Carefully%20plunge%20a%20single%20chitted

How To Grow Potatoes In The Ground | Thompson & Morgan. (n.d.). Www.thompson-Morgan.com. https://www.thompson-morgan.com/how-to-grow-potatoes-in-the-ground

http://www.facebook.com/cultivariable. (2020, January 8). *The Absolute Beginner's Guide to True Potato Seed (TPS) - Cultivariable.* Cultivariable. https://www.cultivariable.com/the-absolute-beginners-guide-to-true-potato-seed-tps/

Jones, A. (2019, August 5). *When and How To Harvest Homegrown Potatoes.* Gardener's Path. https://gardenerspath.com/plants/vegetables/harvest-homegrown-potatoes/

Jones, E. (2020, February 29). *Ultimate Guide to Growing Potatoes in Containers.* Happy DIY Home. https://happydiyhome.com/growing-potatoes-in-containers/

Kendra. (2015, March 25). *How To Plant Potatoes In A Raised Bed.* New Life on a Homestead | Homesteading Blog. https://www.newlifeonahomestead.com/seed-potatoes-and-how-to-plant-potatoes-in-a-raised-bed/

Learn How to Grow Tasty Potatoes in Containers. (n.d.). The Spruce. Retrieved from https://www.thespruce.com/growing-potatoes-in-containers-848220

Lofthouse, J. (n.d.). *Landrace Gardening: True Potato Seeds - Organic Gardening.* Mother Earth News. https://www.motherearthnews.com/organic-gardening/potato-seeds-zbcz1307#:~:text=Potato%20seeds%20are%20harvested%20from

Mother Nature | 3 Ways to Plant Your Potatoes. (2020, April 20). https://mother-nature.ca/3-ways-to-plant-your-potatoes/

Nicholson, B. (2016, March 23). *8 Reasons for Planting Potatoes.* Sun Oven® | the Original Solar Oven & Solar Cooker. https://www.sunoven.com/8-reasons-for-planting-potatoes

Noyes, L. (2019, September 6). *5 Ways To Store Potatoes So They Last For Months.* Rural Sprout. https://www.ruralsprout.com/store-potatoes

Potato | Diseases and Pests, Description, Uses, Propagation. (2013). Psu.edu. https://plantvillage.psu.edu/topics/potato/infos

Raised Bed Garden Design: How To Layout & Build - Garden Design. (n.d.). GardenDesign.com. Retrieved from https://www.gardendesign.com/vegetables/raised-beds.html

StackPath. (n.d.). Www.gardeningknowhow.com. Retrieved from https://www.gardeningknowhow.com/edible/vegetables/potato/growing-potatoes-in-bags.htm

Stradley, L. (2015, May 19). *Potatoes – History of Potatoes.* What's Cooking America. https://whatscookingamerica.net/History/PotatoHistory.htm

The Best 11 Potato Varieties to Grow at Home | Gardener's Path. (2019, October 17). Gardener's Path. https://gardenerspath.com/plants/vegetables/best-potato-varieties/

The Crops Not to Plant After a Potato Crop. (n.d.). Home Guides | SF Gate. https://homeguides.sfgate.com/crops-not-plant-after-potato-crop-54999.html

The Editors of Encyclopedia Britannica. (2018). potato | Definition, Origin, & Facts. In *Encyclopædia Britannica.* https://www.britannica.com/plant/potato

What is a seed potato? (2017, January 4). The Unconventional Gardener. https://theunconventionalgardener.com/blog/seed-potato/

What Kind of Soil Do Potatoes Like? (2013). Sfgate.com. https://homeguides.sfgate.com/kind-soil-potatoes-like-70919.html

What to Spray for Potato Pests. (n.d.). Home Guides | SF Gate. Retrieved from https://homeguides.sfgate.com/spray-potato-pests-48301.html

Made in the USA
Las Vegas, NV
27 August 2023

76705572R00105